OREGON ROAD TRIPS

SOUTHEAST EDITION

Discover Oregon!
Mike + Kristy

MIKE & KRISTY WESTBY

Discover Scenic Backroads & Byways by Day,
Stay in Historic Hotels by Night™

ISBN-13: 978-0998395012

031223 - CS

Cover design by Sarah Craig – SarahCookDesign.com

"Oregon - The Official State of Summer."

FOLLOW DISCOVER-OREGON

On the Web:

www.Discover-Oregon.com

On Twitter:

@DiscoverOre.com

On Facebook:

www.Facebook.com/DiscoverORE

On Instagram:

DiscoverOregon4300

OREGON ROAD TRIPS - SOUTHEAST EDITION

Discover Southeast Oregon!

An exciting 6 to 10-day vacation exploring Southeast Oregon's scenic backroads & byways is now as easy as 1-2-3...

1) Write in the Dates of Your Trip
2) Make Your Historic Hotel Reservations
3) Pack Your Bags and Go!

Using this easy-to-use guide, you'll simply turn each page as you motor along and choose which points of interest to stop at and explore during your day's journey, *all while making your way toward that evening's stay at a historic Oregon hotel.*

An exciting road trip awaits...and it's already planned for you!

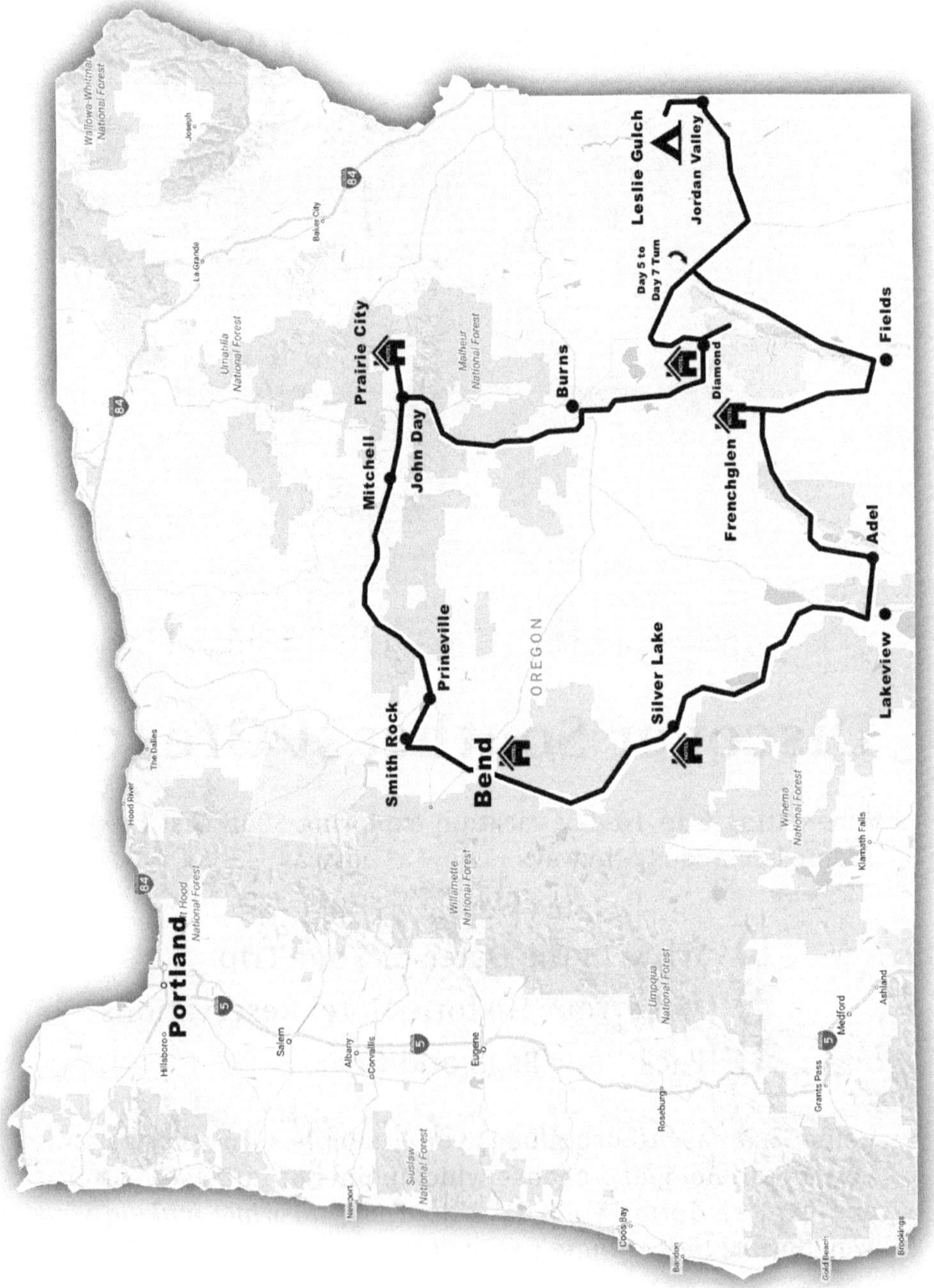
Portland
Bend
Smith Rock
Prineville
Mitchell
John Day
Prairie City
Burns
Diamond
Frenchglen
Fields
Adel
Lakeview
Silver Lake
Leslie Gulch
Jordan Valley
Day 5 to
Day 7 Turn
OREGON
Hillsboro
Salem
Albany
Corvallis
Eugene
Roseburg
Grants Pass
Medford
Ashland
Klamath Falls
Hood River
The Dalles
La Grande
Baker City
Joseph
Newport
Coos Bay
Bandon
Gold Beach
Brookings
Wallowa-Whitman
National Forest
Umatilla
National Forest
Malheur
National Forest
Mt Hood
National Forest
Willamette
National Forest
Siuslaw
National Forest
Umpqua
National Forest
Winema
National Forest
84
5

YOUR JOURNEY

INTRODUCTION

Sheep Rock - John Day Fossil Beds, Oregon

Oregon is a vast and beautiful state. I could list its square mileage, its demographics, or perhaps the distance from border to border, but a better description is...it starts with the shores of the Pacific Ocean on its western edge, traverses east over the Oregon Coast Range and into the verdant Willamette Valley, climbs over the snowy summits of the Cascade mountain range while skirting south of the sublime Columbia River Gorge and then continues forever into the remote, silent and dramatic beauty and history of eastern Oregon.

This guide is about setting out on your own adventure to explore Oregon. It's about the journey, not the destination. It's about asking, "I wonder where that goes?" It's about hitting the brakes and turning left onto a gravel road. Opening a door and saying "Hello". Shutting off the engine, getting out of the car and listening to the silence of distance. It's about the angry tug on a fly line, wondering just how many stars a sky can hold, and what would really happen, I mean *really* happen, if you just kept going.

Recently, my wife, Kristy, and I set out on a nine-day 1,409 mile journey along the backroads and byways of Southeast Oregon to discover its intriguing sites, small towns and scenic wonders, all while staying in historic hotels each evening. Our goal was to stop and explore all of the places we normally rush past when we're traveling, because we're in such a hurry to reach our destination. As we met folks along the way, we were surprised by how many said they've always wanted to make a similar trip but they didn't know where or how to begin planning it, and this was usually followed by a request for a copy of our itinerary once we finished our journey. We decided to go one step further and write up our notes, add some photos, include some maps and turn it all into an easy-to-use guidebook so that others could duplicate our trip with little effort, all while customizing it to their own interests and sense of adventure.

How To Begin

Oregon's immense size, historical treasures and abundance of geographical features are too much to capture in one trip. In fact, its countless riches can be so intimidating that travelers don't know where to begin...so they don't.

Good news! This book already has your route planned for you. There are only three simple things you need to do...

1) Select the 6 to 10-day period for your road trip and write those dates into this book at the beginning of each chapter.

2) Call and make reservations at the historic hotels found at the end of each day, which correspond with your chosen dates.

3) Pack your bags, hop in the car and simply choose the sights you wish to stop at and explore each day as you motor along. It's that easy!

Note that some of the optional activities you'll enjoy during your trip, such as river rafting on the Deschutes, viewing the Kam Wah Chung Museum, or enjoying dinner at the Cowboy Dinner Tree will also require reservations, and these are noted at the beginning of each chapter/day.

Where to Begin

Your road trip begins with a day (or two) of adventure in Bend, before proceeding east into the "Oregon Frontier" of eastern Central Oregon. From there, you'll turn south to explore the remote regions and geologic wonders of southeastern Oregon.

We recommend you begin by spending the first two nights of your trip in Bend, at the historic McMenamins Old St. Francis School. Formerly a 1936 Catholic schoolhouse, today its renovated classrooms have been converted into a 60-room hotel, restaurant, brewery, pub, live music venue, theatre, and more, all with a friendly one-of-a-kind atmosphere.

Where to Finish

Your Southeast Oregon road trip begins with one full day / two nights in Bend. However, you may want to seriously consider adding a few days on the front or back end of your road trip to explore all of the outdoor fun and adventure Bend has to offer. Hiking, mountain biking, road cycling, paddleboarding, kayaking, fishing, rock climbing, river floating, skiing, dining, shopping, and much, much more await you. See pages 14 and 64 to learn more about extending your road trip.

Central Oregon - An Explorer's Guide

In addition to this book, we're also authors of the *Central Oregon - An Explorer's Guide,* which reveals over 200 things to See, Do & Explore throughout *all* of Central Oregon. It's the perfect guidebook to use as a reference should you decide to extend your trip with a few more days in Bend. To learn more about our book, see page 179.

Parking Permits

Central and Southeast Oregon are a mix of National Forests, State Parks, National Monuments, BLM land, and private property. Many of these areas provide free access, but you may choose to visit some sites during your road trip which require either an Oregon State Parks or National Forest parking pass. You'll find most of these are located in the Bend area. Depending upon the number of sites you choose to visit during your trip which require a permit, you may be fine with buying daily parking passes at the sites you're visiting, instead of buying an annual pass beforehand. You'll find additional information about these passes and where they are required throughout this book.

Northwest Forest Pass - Annual Northwest Forest Passes may be purchased at numerous outdoor retailers, including REI, various ranger stations, or online. To learn which sites and trailheads require a pass or to purchase a pass online, Google "Northwest Forest Pass" with your web browser online.

Oregon State Parks Day-Use Parking Permit - Daily: $5 - Annual: $30 - This permit is honored at all 26 Oregon State

Parks which charge a parking fee. Permits are available at self-service kiosks, park booths, or offices located at the site in which a permit is required. In addition, they may be purchased by calling 800-551-6949 or online at https://www.oregonstateparks.org. Note that if you purchase a *daily* parking permit at one site in Oregon, you may use that permit at any other site in Oregon that requires the same permit *for the remainder of that day.* You do not need to buy a new permit at each site.

Black & White Photos

So, what's up with the black and white photos instead of color?

Well, we'd *really* like to use color photos throughout our guide. Seriously, that would be great! However, in order to reach economies of scale and keep the book affordable if we were to use color photos, we'd have to print thousands of copies at a time. That's all well and fine, but it would mean that we couldn't make any updates to this guidebook until all of those copies were sold, which would take years. What kind of updates are we talking about? Well, in the past year alone, we've twice updated the information found throughout the guidebook, significantly updated all of the maps, reviewed and updated information for the most remote parts of the road trip, added new destinations and photos, and more.

In order to regularly make updates, we use print-on-demand technology to print much smaller runs of books at a time. The only downside is that if we were to use color photos with POD technology, the costs involved with using color with these smaller print runs would make this guidebook prohibitively expensive, so the compromise is...black and white photos...but with up-to-date information.

Yo, No Quid Pro Quo

As you use this guidebook, you'll notice that we mention many different restaurants, hotels, museums, attractions, and other retail destinations all throughout the guide itself and within its back pages. We'd like you to know that none of these destinations have paid to be included within our guidebook, nor provided us with any form of compensation. We have included them only because we thought you'd like to know about them, they add to your Southeast Oregon road trip experience, and we're big fans of small businesses and the entrepreneurial spirit.

One Last Thing

Although we go to great lengths to verify the accuracy of the information contained within this guidebook, the dynamic world you're about to road trip into is always changing. Restaurants and retail stores can close without notice, hotels may change their hours, road signs could disappear for a variety of reasons, or an always open gate may be locked shut. In addition, the weather and seasons may make some roads impassable at times. If you're uncomfortable with or unskilled in dealing with the out-of-doors and the unforeseen challenges travelers can sometimes face there, you may wish to avoid this trip. With that in mind, no responsibility is assumed on our part for any errors or omissions of information contained within this guidebook, and no liability is assumed for damages or injury that may result from the use of the information contained herein.

MAKE YOUR RESERVATIONS

The 1923 Frenchglen Hotel - Frenchglen, Oregon

These are the reservations you will need to make for your road trip. All necessary lodging reservations are shown in bold. All others are optional activities.

Day 1 - Arrive At Bend, Oregon

- **Stay at the McMenamins Old St. Francis School - 541-382-5174**
  - Make reservations for 2 Nights
    - *Consider making reservations at this time for any additional days you'd like to spend exploring Bend and the surrounding area either before or after your road trip.*

- In addition, Bend offers a wealth of other lodging accommodations, and you'll find more information about these on page 65.

Day 2 - Spend the Day Exploring Bend, Oregon

Spend your second night at McMenamins Old St. Francis School

Day 3 - Bend, OR to Prairie City, OR

Make a reservation for 1 night

- **Historic Hotel Prairie - 541-820-4800**

Day 4 - Prairie City, OR to Diamond, OR

Make a reservation for 1 night

- **Historic Hotel Diamond - 541-493-1898**
- Hotel Dinner Reservations - 6:30 pm
    - Strongly recommended, as there are no other dining options in Diamond

Day 5 - Diamond, OR to Leslie Gulch

You are camping this evening - No reservations required

Day 6 - Explore Leslie Gulch

Spend a second night camping at Leslie Gulch

Day 7 - Leslie Gulch to Frenchglen, OR

Make a reservation for 2 Nights

- **Frenchglen Hotel - 541-493-2825**
- Hotel Dinner Reservations - 6:30 pm
    - Strongly recommended, as there are no other dining options in Frenchglen

Day 8 - Explore Steens Mountain

Spend your second night at the Frenchglen Hotel

Day 9 - Frenchglen, OR to Silver Lake, OR

Make a reservation for 1 night

- **Lodging at Cowboy Dinner Tree - 541-576-2426**
- Dinner Reservations at Cowboy Dinner Tree (Required)

Day 10 - Silver Lake, OR to Home

If You Spend Any Additional Days in Bend

Reservations are required for any of the following optional activities in Bend or the surrounding area:

- Rafting - Sun Country Tours - 541-382-1709
    - Be sure to bring water shoes and a swim suit for this activity. Learn more on page 45.

- Bike Rentals - See Page 50.

SOME GROUND RULES

"It's the Journey, Not the Destination."

The key to your journey is to alter your driving mindset. It really isn't about getting *there*, it's about discovering *here*. With this in mind, here are some ground rules to follow...

- Get used to stopping the car and getting out.
- Now stop the car and get out.
- Stop the car and get out...again. You'll be glad you did.
- Always ask "I wonder where that goes?"...and go there.
- Hit the brakes and turn left.
- Open the door and say "Hello."
- Don't assume it has to be a short conversation.
- Never mind that you just stopped back there...stop again here.
- Yes, it is a nice view. Feel free to stop, get out and admire it.
- Always remember that this very moment is the time to do it. You won't be coming back this way next week.
- Enjoy the journey!

Travel Beyond the Page

By all means, do not feel you have to stop at only the places found in this book, as there are many more than those listed here just waiting to be discovered. Go ahead...follow that dusty road, stop at that small museum, visit the town's old cemetery, and walk that trail to the viewpoint. It's all about taking the time to...discover Oregon.

The Same, But Different

Following the information in this guide, you will enjoy a unique and exciting road trip discovering Southeast Oregon. It's important to note, however, that with a little creativity you can also make this same journey a second or third time and have it be an almost entirely new and different trip each time. With trip number one, you may find you have only enough time in your day to explore Smith Rock State Park, the Painted Hills, Kam Wah Chung State Heritage Site and Owyhee Canyon Overlook, leaving the Pete French Round Barn, Leslie Gulch, Steins Pillar, and Crack in the Ground completely undiscovered. That means they'll all be waiting for you when you make your next trip!

"So, Where Are You From?"

There are many blessings on a trip like this, one of which is the number of conversations you simply fall into. It usually begins with a simple question or comment, and the next thing you know you're involved in a 30-minute conversation with some of the nicest people you've ever met. Why? Because the folks you meet on a trip like this are your neighbors, it's just that they're a quite a few houses further down the block. If you approach a town, café, museum or someone with an air of traveling arrogance, then you're making a huge mistake. Instead, be genuine and friendly. You'll be amazed at how many people you'll meet and how pleasant your trip will be.

And in those rare instances where you meet someone who loves to talk...about themselves...then excuse yourselves with the tried and true "Well, we need to be hitting the road if we're going to stay on schedule."

The Right Frame of Mind

During your journey, your mindset will make all the difference between having an amazing trip filled with fond memories that will last a lifetime or a less-than-stellar odyssey you'd just as soon forget. Is the single-pane window in your 1920s era hotel room a bit drafty? Then it's historically accurate, not in need of replacement. Did you come out to your car one morning only to find a flat tire? Find a helpful Les Schwab Tire Store and be thankful it's not a broken spoke on a wagon wheel. Did the local steakhouse close early because business was kind of slow today? Then that's exactly a taste of the slower pace of life you were seeking. Always go with the flow, and you'll be happy you did.

Get Some Good *Paper* Maps

We can't emphasize this enough. You will want to travel with and use a couple of good paper maps, and the more detailed, the better. Your phone or similar device will no doubt work well, but you're setting out to explore some very remote parts of Oregon, many of which have no cell signal whatsoever, so your phone will not work there. In addition, your paper maps will always boot up and never run out of power.

As you make your way along your journey and stop at various locations, you'll often see folded Oregon maps made available for free by the Oregon Department of Transportation. These are very helpful, so grab more than one and keep them with you at all times. For more detail on the backroads you'll be traveling, we also recommend the large Oregon atlases put out by DeLorme. These are excellent tools, and you can find them online for about $25.

Oregon's tourism division, Travel Oregon, also issues very helpful maps, magazines and trip guides. We highly recommend you visit their web site, www.TravelOregon.com, to order some of these guides before setting out on your trip. Especially helpful is their large *Oregon Scenic Byways Official Driving Guide.*

If you are a member of AAA, check their resources, as well. By the way, make sure your membership is up-to-date.

The Time of Year Makes a Difference

Your Southeast Oregon road trip is best made during mid-spring to late fall, when temperatures are warm, the days are longer and the higher elevation roads are clear of snow and winter debris. Most roads are open year-round, but portions of higher elevation roads, such as the Steens Mountain Loop Tour Route, are closed due to snow in the early spring. Plan on most routes being snow free sometime in mid- to late May, though this can vary. (Steens Mountain often opens on the July 4th weekend) If you're traveling during this time, call the corresponding Ranger Stations to get the latest road status. *Travel tools, such as a small shovel and bow saw, may come in very handy when traveling early in the year.*

Note that the mid-summer months of July and August can be very warm in the central and southeast sections of Oregon, with temperatures sometimes reaching well into the 90s. Be sure to travel with plenty of water.

Be Prepared

Be self-sufficient as you travel along, as some areas are very remote. Be sure to bring extra food, drinks, a first-aid kit, a roadside emergency kit, jumper cables, a phone charger with cables, a tire inflator, (yes, I've had to use one!) a blanket, maps, a small shovel, flashlights with fresh batteries, a lighter, a whistle, road flares and a small tarp to sit upon should you have to change a tire or dig out from some snow. Note that should you experience some kind of difficulties while on the road, chances are someone will be along soon.

Don't Get Stuck

It is widely known by the locals in Southeast Oregon that you do not drive on dirt roads if it has recently rained or is going to do so in the near future. The rain mixes with the dust to create very slippery conditions, and you will get stuck. You will then have to wait until things dry out before you can continue. Well maintained gravel roads should be fine, however.

Check Jordan Valley, OR

FYI, you'll want to check the current status of the restaurants (and lodging, if you choose not to camp in Leslie Gulch) in Jordan Valley, OR prior to departing for your trip. Restaurants tend to come and go without notice in this small town in remote southeast Oregon.

Six Hours Per Day – Your Results May Vary

As we've said, it's all about the journey and not the destination. That said, we found that after about six hours of being on the road, we were flipping this mantra and were ready to reach our destination. Our willingness to stop and explore was being replaced by a desire to simply reach our hotel, relax and "be there." Everybody's results will certainly vary, but we found that about six hours on the road was enough for a day.

Bring Some Binoculars

From dramatic geologic features and wide open vistas to circling hawks and perhaps even a bear, there is much to see during your Southeast Oregon road trip, so you may want to consider bringing along a good pair of binoculars for use throughout your journey.

Les Schwab Tire Centers

If you're on the road and have a flat tire, brake issues or a similar problem, we highly recommend the very helpful and nice folks at your nearby Les Schwab Tire Centers, which are located throughout Oregon. You'll find phone numbers for multiple locations on Page 172.

We'd Love to Hear About Your Trip!

We know you're out there, having fun while "out in the field" discovering Oregon with this book in hand, and we'd love to hear about your exploits! Drop us a note anytime and let us know...What kind of fun are you having? Where did you go? What did you like best? What did you not like at all? What do you think we should add to this book? Feel free to send us a note or a photo at ContactUs@Discover-Oregon.com. We'd love to hear how it went.

You'll be Camping for 2 Nights...or Not

This Discover Oregon road trip involves two nights of camping at Leslie Gulch in far Southeast Oregon. We're assuming you're familiar with the art of camping and have all of the proper equipment. If you're not, then you have a couple of options;

1) Instead of camping in Leslie Gulch, reserve a room for two nights in Jordan Valley, which is 50 miles south of Leslie Gulch. Then, on the morning of Day 6, drive north to Leslie Gulch to explore the area during the day before returning back to your lodging in Jordan Valley that evening. You would be staying in Jordan Valley for the nights of Day 5 and Day 6.

   Note: With the Covid-19 pandemic, your best lodging option in Jordan Valley, the Flat Iron Steakhouse Inn, closed and was no longer accepting guests. Rumor has it, however, that it may reopen after the pandemic. As of the publication of this edition in 2023, it is not known if this will happen or under what name the inn may reopen. *See pages 105 & 109 for additional information.*

2) If you prefer not to camp nor drive to Jordan Valley and Leslie Gulch at all, you may skip that leg of your trip by departing from the Pete French Round Barn on Day 5 and jumping directly to mid-day on Day 7, where you'll turn south off of Highway 78 and travel along Fields-Denio Road / East Steens Road Tour Route toward Fields, OR before turning north to your evening's stay at the historic Frenchglen Hotel in Frenchglen, Oregon. See the maps on pages 6 & 104 and information on pages 129 and 130 for details and directions. Note that this will shorten your road trip by two days.

Days One & Two

Travel to & Explore Bend, OR

Days 1 & 2
Travel To & Explore Bend

Days 1 & 2 – Dates: / / - / /

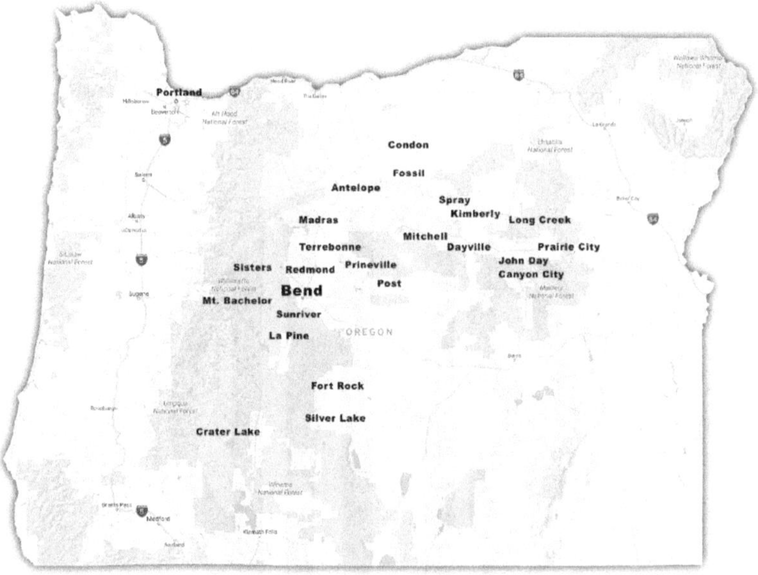

Summary: Where You're Going Today

- Arrive and spend days 1 & 2 of your road trip exploring Bend and the surrounding area

Today, you begin your Southeast Oregon road trip by driving to Bend. (Day 1 of your road trip.) You'll definitely want to arrive early enough to take advantage of the abundance of outdoor activities Bend has to offer, and you will seriously want to consider adding to your road trip by arriving a day or two or three early to explore even more of Bend and the surrounding area, or choose to stay a few days after your road trip. With additional time, you could make a trip out to Sisters, raft Big Eddy on the Deschutes River, drive to the top of 7,984' Paulina Peak, hike to a waterfall, ride a summer chairlift up Mt.

Bachelor, hike all the way around Smith Rock, and so much more. For a complete description of over 200 things to See, Do & Explore in Bend and *all* of Central Oregon, you may also want to consider our book, *Central Oregon - An Explorer's Guide.* (The Bend content within the following pages is from this guide.) See page 179 for additional details.

Tonight's Lodging:

- McMenamins Old St. Francis School - 541-382-5174
  - Make a reservation for 2 nights

- Important: Note that you'll begin your road trip by making lodging reservations at McMenamins in Bend for your *first two nights.* (Your day of arrival and one full day exploring Bend.) On Day 10 of your road trip, you may choose to finish your trip back in Bend instead of heading home. If you'd like to remain in Bend for a few more days *after* your road trip to explore more of Bend's many adventures and activities, which appear on the following pages, then you'll want to make reservations for those nights now, as well. See page 64 for additional details.

- Note: You can use the Bend activities information that appears on the following pages as a guidebook for your additional days spent exploring Bend.

Today's Mileage: Varies based upon your departure point for your trip to Bend today.

(Optional) Reservations Needed for This Segment:

- Raft the Deschutes River
  - Sun Country Tours - 541-382-1709

- Bike Rentals
  - Pine Mountain Sports - 541-385-8080
  - Hutch's Bicycles - 541-382-9253
  - Web Cyclery - 541-318-6188

- Sunset Dinner on Mt. Bachelor - 541-382-1709

Explore Bend, OR

Located near the center of Oregon, at the transition point between the snow-covered Cascade Mountains to the west and the high-desert to the east, Bend offers visitors an abundance of outdoor activities and adventures, all complemented with spectacular scenery. Here, your days can be filled with hiking, mountain biking, road cycling, kayaking, paddleboarding, rock climbing, mountaineering, skiing, fly fishing, or even shopping, catching a movie, and exploring a local museum, while your evenings top off your day with great food, cold microbrews, live music, and maybe even a moonlight kayaking session on a high alpine lake. *Photo © Nate Wyeth*

Explore Bend: Old Mill District

Formerly home to two massive lumber mills located on opposite banks of the Deschutes River, today the site hosts the Old Mill District shopping area offering visitors the choice of over 50 different tax-free shops and restaurants, including REI, The Confluence Fly Shop, Savory Spice, Naked Winery, and Victoria's Secret, as well as outdoor concerts at the Hayden Homes Amphitheater, ice cream at Ben & Jerry's, first-run movies at the Old Mill theater, First Friday Art Walks, scenic strolls along the slow-flowing Deschutes River, and more. This is a great place to spend a summer afternoon as you watch people float by on their inner tubes or catch a wave at the nearby Bend Whitewater Park, before enjoying dinner while experiencing a beautiful sunset over the mountains to the west.

By the way, watching the river surfers from the bridge at the Bend Whitewater Park just downriver from the Old Mill District is a "must do" activity. They're fun to watch, and they surf year-round in all temperatures, even when it is freezing cold out. To reach the water park, simply hike the paved trail along the Deschutes downriver ¼ mile from the Old Mill District.

Explore Bend: Hayden Homes Amphitheater

Imagine it's a beautiful summer evening, you're sitting on soft cool grass, one of your favorite bands is playing live music on an outdoor stage, and the sun is lighting a fire in the clouds over the Cascades as it drifts below the horizon to make room for a night sky full of stars. That is a concert at the Hayden Homes Amphitheater. Located along the Deschutes in the Old Mill District, the amphitheater is host to performers such as Lyle Lovett, Pink Martini, Chris Stapleton, The Roots, Ziggy Marley, and many others, as well as race events and the second largest beer fest in the Pacific Northwest, showcasing three days of "craft beer bliss." Check the amphitheater's event schedule online to see who will be performing while you're in town and reserve your seats! *Photo © Matthew Lasala*

Hayden Homes Amphitheater
344 SW Shevlin Hixon Drive
Bend, OR 97702

Explore Bend: Bend Whitewater Park

A few years ago, the Deschutes river beneath the SW Colorado Avenue bridge was blocked with a weir made up of large boulders, thus creating an obstruction that was extremely dangerous to paddleboarders, kayakers, river floaters, and others who were forced to exit the river above the weir and walk around it with all of their gear so as to continue downriver.

Today, the weir and its dangerous boulders have been removed and replaced with a very popular whitewater park that now allows users to easily drift through this section of the river in a series of fun and exciting drops, as well as practice surfing on a permanent wave, a feature that is always busy with surfers, even during the winter months!

Make your way to McKay park immediately downriver from The Old Mill and stand on the SW Colorado Avenue bridge as you watch all of the surfers, kayakers, paddleboarders, and river floaters enjoy the summer (and winter!) fun.

Can't make it to the park today? Then check out the EyeOnBend.com web cam site, which has a web cam trained on the whitewater park and river surfers.

Bend Whitewater Park
166 SW Shevlin Hixon Dr.
Bend, OR 97702

Explore Bend: Shopping Downtown Bend

Enjoy wandering through small shops or grab a bite to eat while shopping in historic downtown Bend. Located primarily on Wall and Bond streets, small businesses offer the creative wares of local artisans, craftspeople, authors, jewelers and more, all in a welcoming small town atmosphere. Shop for housewares, Bend-inspired apparel, artwork, a new favorite wine, the perfect novel to enjoy during your stay, or even a big ice cream sundae with sprinkles on top!

Explore Bend: First Friday Art Walk

During the first Friday of every month, dozens of Bend retailers, including boutiques, bookstores, shops, galleries, restaurants, and more showcase the creative artistic works of local and regional artists as part of the First Friday Art Walk. Stroll from shop to shop to meet the artists, see the exhibits, listen to live music, and enjoy good food and wine. The event is free to the public and held in downtown Bend, as well as at the historic Old Mill District.

Smith Rock artwork by Sheila Dunn. See her outstanding work at www.SheilaDunnArt.com

Explore Bend: Northwest Crossing Saturday Farmers Market

Start your Saturday off with the fun and festive Northwest Crossing Saturday Farmers Market. Stroll among a large collection of vendors offering fresh local produce, baked goods, vibrant flowers, artisan crafts and jewelry, hand-crafted furniture, and even flavored vodkas. Then enjoy a bite for lunch from one of the handful of food carts while you enjoy live music.

- The market runs from 10:00 a.m. to 2:00 p.m. on Saturdays from early June through late September. It is closed on Sundays.

Northwest Crossing Saturdays Farmers Market
NW Crossing Drive
Bend, OR 97703

Explore Bend: Central Oregon Saturday Market

Explore the many booths of the Central Oregon Saturday Market. Here, you'll discover an abundance of goods created by local and regional artisans, including pottery, artwork, photography, clothing, yard art, homeware, hand-crafted furniture, woodwork, lavender oils and soaps, jewelry, and even items for man's best friend.

The market runs every Saturday from 10:00 a.m. to 4:00 p.m., from Memorial Day Weekend in June through Labor Day Weekend in September. It is closed on Sundays. Note, however, that it is open on both Saturday and Sunday on its opening and closing weekends only.

Located Across from the Deschutes Public Library
Wall Street
Bend, OR 97703
650-771-3544

Explore Bend: Tower Theatre

Built in 1940, the beautifully restored Tower Theatre in "old town" Bend welcomes guests with an ever-changing variety of offerings, including concerts, speakers, dramas, comedies, documentaries, varied events, and of course films, all hosted in a grand and elegant Art Deco ambiance. See what's playing during your visit by visiting their web site online.

Tower Theatre
835 NW Wall Street
Bend, OR 97701
541-317-0700

Explore Bend: Bonta Natural Artisan Gelato

You'll want to stop in at Bonta Natural Artisan Gelato while you're shopping in downtown Bend, before catching a movie at the nearby Tin Pan Theater, or perhaps even as an after dinner treat. Sit on a bench outside and people watch as you enjoy a delicious cone of salted chocolate, hazelnut, vanilla bourbon pecan or any of their 18 signature flavors of gelato, all made fresh using local natural ingredients and served with a smile.

"If we can't pronounce it, it doesn't go into our ice cream."

Bonta Natural Artisan Gelato
920 NW Bond Street - Ste 108
(Entrance is on Minnesota Ave.)
Bend, OR 97701

- Open: Monday through Sunday

Explore Bend: Tin Pan Theater

Poorly marked and down a non-descript alleyway in downtown Bend is the quaint Tin Pan Theater. Step through the doorway and enter the best show in town with only 28 seats, a small "big screen" and a bar serving drinks, snacks, and food. Here, you'll typically find movies that aren't playing at the local Cine-plex, but instead award-winning films, documentaries, classics, and more. Even better, in the summer they host "spaghetti westerns", at which they show old-fashioned western films...while serving spaghetti from the bar!

Tin Pan Theater
869 Northwest Tin Pan Alley
Bend, OR 97703
541-241-2271

Note: If you're a bit on the bashful side, use the restroom before you leave home. It's not that the restroom at the Tin Pan Theater is bad, it's just that the door opens right next to the screen up front, where you become part of the show.

Explore Bend: Cravin's Candy Emporium

Enjoy a sweet blast to the past at Cravin's Candy Emporium in downtown Bend. You'll find every possible kind of candy from your youth, as well as all of today's favorites. Candies from every decade reaching back to 1900 fill the store, including Atomic Fireballs, Black Licorice Pipes, Root Beer Barrels, Whistle Pops, Pop Rocks, Chick-O-Sticks, Wax Lips and more.

Cravin's Candy Emporium
818 NW Wall Street
Bend, OR 97701
541-617-9866

Explore Bend: Drake Park

Located on the banks of the Deschutes River and just west of "Old Town" Bend, 13-acre Drake Park is the perfect (and popular) place to take a stroll while capturing the essence of Bend life as you watch the Deschutes slowly flow by. Walk through the cool grass in the shade of towering Ponderosa Pines, find a park bench and enjoy an ice cream cone, or sit for a while in the sun as you watch ducks and Canada Geese busily upend into the water to nibble the tender plants just below the surface. In the summer, the park is home to all kinds of events, art and craft fairs, concerts, festivals, and more.

Explore Bend: Deschutes Historical Museum

Dedicated to preserving the history of Central Oregon and the surrounding area, the Deschutes Historical Museum welcomes visitors with an impressive collection of artifacts and exhibits reflecting Central Oregon's multi-faceted history. Visit the museum to learn about the growth of the skiing and recreational industry in Central Oregon, the important role logging played in driving the region's economy, the life of the Native Americans and early pioneers in the area, the fascinating story behind the fierce competition to bring the first rail line to Bend, and more.

Deschutes Historical Museum
129 NW Idaho Ave.
Bend, OR 97701
541-389-1813

Explore Bend: Pilot Butte Summit

Visible from most anywhere in town, 500' high Pilot Butte is the large cinder cone located in east Bend. You'll find both a one-mile spiraling trail and paved road winding their way up through juniper and sage brush on the butte's flanks before cresting at the top. Once you reach the summit, you'll be rewarded with an amazing 360 degree panoramic vista of central Oregon with outstanding views of the Cascade peaks in the distance and Bend at your feet. The road is popular with runners, and the top is an excellent place to watch a sunset. Bring a headlamp if you are hiking back down after dark.

Note: The top of Pilot Butte is also the stage for Bend's 4th of July fireworks display. Fireworks are fired from the summit, which everyone for miles and miles around can see and enjoy. If you're in town over the 4th, you'll want to scout a good location for watching these prior to the evening of the 4th.

Explore Bend: Shevlin Park Trails

Located less than three miles from Bend, Shevlin Park in Northwest Bend is the "go-to" place for a casual yet adventurous outing. Popular with families, groups, and individuals, it's a large forested park offering hikes along the small Tumalo River, mountain bike riding on forested hillsides, jogging on shaded paths, fly fishing, picnicking, benches along the river, and more. And with its Larch and Aspen trees, it is a beautiful park to hike during the fall colors in September and October.

Shevlin Park
18920 NW Shevlin Park Road
Bend, OR 97701
541-389-7275

Explore Bend: Riley Ranch Nature Reserve

Perfect for a sunny day, the 184-acre Riley Ranch Nature Reserve in Northwest Bend does an outstanding job of showcasing some of the diverse landscapes and ecosystems found throughout Bend and Central Oregon. Take the short Juniper Trail right out of the parking area to walk amongst gnarled ancient Juniper Trees before moving on to the Sage Flat Loop Trail, which surrounds a large open meadow highlighted by the Sage Flat Overlook. Then make your way over to the nearby Canyon

Overlook, a large observation deck set atop a long rimrock cliff and offering views deep into a rocky canyon below. Standing here, you can listen to the Deschutes River as it flows past the lower section of the reserve, home to the Canyon Loop Trail, which connects to Tumalo State Park, just to the north. Note that the Robin's Run Trail at the northern end of the upper portion of the reserve will connect you to the lower portion down in the canyon.

The entire reserve is bisected by short hiking loops consisting of wide mostly level crushed gravel paths, and when connected together in a variety of combinations, they offer a hike as short or as long as you'd like.

- Open sunrise to sunset.
- An easy year-round trail with little elevation gain or loss, unless you drop down into the canyon.
- Dogs and bikes are not allowed.

Riley Ranch Nature Reserve
19975 Glen Vista Road
Bend, OR 97701

Explore Bend: The Deschutes River Trail

The beautiful Deschutes River cuts its way for 252 miles through Central Oregon, from its headwaters at Little Lava Lake to its confluence with the Mighty Columbia River at Oregon's northern border. As it passes through Bend and the surrounding area, the Deschutes is often flanked by multiple sections of the Deschutes River Trail, an extremely popular trail system used by walkers, runners, hikers, families with strollers, and many others. The flavor of the trail changes considerably as it passes along different stretches of the river, including a retail area at The Old Mill, and it is a scenic and enjoyable walk anytime of the day, but especially during the nice lighting of the morning and late afternoon. Here are three of our favorite stretches to get you started exploring...

Deschutes River Trail - Farewell Bend Park Trailhead

Find your way to Farewell Bend Park and walk the trail upriver on the north or south bank of the Deschutes for approximately 1.5 miles to a footbridge spanning the river. Cross here and then hike back to the park on the opposite bank. Make a point to find a high cliffside or rocky outcropping on the river itself to sit and enjoy the view, and to perhaps spot some kayakers navigating the whitewater, which can be anytime of the year. When you're finished, walk over to The Old Mill and enjoy an ice cream cone at Ben & Jerry's!

- An easy year-round trail with little elevation gain.
- Park at Farewell Bend Park, and you'll find the trail near the river's edge. This trail is also known as Deschutes River Trail South.
- Dogs are permitted while on a leash.
- Bikes are permitted on the trail along the south side of the river, but not on the north side.
- A parking permit is not required to park at Farewell Bend Park.

Farewell Bend Park
1000 SW Reed Market Road
Bend, OR 97702

Deschutes River Trail - Tumalo State Park Trailhead

Here's a stretch of the Deschutes River Trail that is filled with character, seeming to offer a little bit of everything. Leave from the southernmost parking area of Tumalo State Park and start with a nice hike next to the river, perhaps offering a wave to a couple of kayakers as they drift past, before beginning to ascend into the forest where you'll soon come upon an interesting boardwalk (0.8 miles) which carries you across a wide talus field of large boulders while offering a nice view of the river below. Continue on to spot the confluence of Tumalo Creek with The Deschutes across the way before reaching the lower canyon portion of the Riley Ranch Nature Reserve. Walk past the entrance sign and map to explore a level path through a shady forest while making your way to a small rocky butte as part of the Canyon Loop Trail. Along the way, you'll pass the ruins of a log cabin and outbuilding, which were likely built sometime in the 1800s. Choose to hike the Canyon Loop back to the entrance of the reserve, or take the short trail to the top of a small butte where you'll find a nice bench to sit upon and enjoy the view. You brought your lunch, didn't you? BTW, the viewing platform you see across the canyon is part of the upper portion of the Riley Ranch Nature Reserve. (Page 38)

- An easy year-round trail with little elevation gain.
- Approximately 2.6 miles to the small butte on the Canyon Loop.
- Dogs are not permitted at the Riley Ranch Nature Reserve.
- An Oregon State Parks parking permit is required to park at Tumalo State Park. A daily

parking permit may also be purchased at the automated kiosk at the park entrance.
- If you are hiking in the afternoon, make a note of when the park entrance gate closes for the day.
- You'll find the trailhead at the south end of the southernmost parking lot.

Tumalo State Park
64170 O.B. Riley Road
Tumalo, OR 97703

Deschutes River Trail - Sawyer Park to Archie Briggs Canyon

Walk a broad graveled trail dotted with interpretive signs that point out that you're actually walking atop a large irrigation pipeline out to the Archie Briggs Natural Area, an area frequented by more than 140 species of birds, including Bald Eagles, Belted Kingfishers, Western Osprey, Song Sparrows, Western Wood-Peewees, and more. Making its way next to the Deschutes River below, the path is very popular with walkers, runners, and cyclists. Park at Sawyer Park, cross the large footbridge across the Deschutes, and take the broad path that leads to your right. There are a lot of paths in this area, both large and small, which all tend to lead to the river or elsewhere, but if you stay on the broad packed graveled path, it will lead you up to the Deschutes River Trail. Follow this north for a little over one mile (or more, if you choose) to the Archie Briggs Natural Area. The Deschutes River Trail and Sawyer Park are open year-round, but the park is open daily from sunrise to sunset.

- An easy year-round trail with little elevation gain.
- Up to 5 miles round-trip.
- Dogs are permitted while on a leash.
- There is no charge for parking at Sawyer Park.

Note that this section of the Deschutes River Trail also makes for a nice casual mountain bike ride.

Sawyer Park
62999 O.B. Riley Road
Bend, OR 97701
541-389-7275

Explore Bend: Ice Skating - The Pavilion

If you're ready for some ice skating fun...on a NHL-sized ice rink, then you'll want to head to the ice rink at The Pavilion. Take some lessons, let go of the railing, and try a triple salchow!

The "ice season" runs from October through April, and the rink is typically open from 8:00 a.m. to 8:00 p.m., though it is used for different activities throughout the day, including open skates, family skates, adult skates, lessons, hockey games, freestyle figure skating, and curling. Visit the Bend Parks and Rec web site online to see the current rink schedule.

The Pavilion
1001 Southwest Bradbury Way
Bend, OR 97702
541-389-7588
Info@BendParksandRec.org

Explore Bend: Ice Skating - Seventh Mountain Resort

Take to the ice in an old-fashioned setting outdoors under the Ponderosa Pines at Seventh Mountain Resort. Open to the public, their quaint rink is the perfect size for a memorable skate under the stars of a clear night sky...or a bright afternoon sun. Afterwards, enjoy a hot chocolate and tasty treat to keep you warm. If you time it right, you can join in on the Christmas celebrations when the resort's festive Christmas tree is lit early in December, or when Santa takes to the ice later in the month. Visit their web site at www.SeventhMountain.com/Recreation/ or call 541-693-9124 to find the current hours and pricing. The "ice season" is from early December to March 1st. Skate rentals are also available.

Seventh Mountain Resort Ice Rink
18575 SW Century Drive
Bend, OR 97702
541-693-9124
www.SeventhMountain.com/Recreation/

Explore Bend: Visit Bend - Bend Visitor Center

You'll find information on many different things to see, do, and explore in Bend and the surrounding area within this guide, but if you want to learn about Bend's many restaurants and breweries, the different events occurring throughout the year, summer concerts, winter activities, where to stay, or even the Bend Ale Trail, then stop in at Visit Bend.

Here, you'll find helpful guides, maps, event schedules, advice, and the perfect Bend souvenir.

Visit Bend - Bend Visitor Center
750 NW Lava Road, Ste 160
Bend, OR 97703
877-245-8484
541-382-8048
www.VisitBend.com

Explore Bend: Rafting and Floating the Deschutes River

Perhaps you've seen kayakers or rafters taking on the challenge of navigating rapids on the Deschutes River and thought you'd like to give it a try. Well, now's your chance. Rafting down the churning whitewater of the Big Eddy rapid is a guaranteed highlight of your road trip! In addition to kayaking on the Deschutes, we've rafted Big Eddy several times, and it's always the perfect summertime thrill for everyone in the family.

You won't be doing this on your own, however. Instead, you'll sign up with Sun Country Tours, and they'll take care of everything. Visit their web site to make your reservations, and then check in at their office just off of 14th street on the big day. You'll board their former school bus and ride to the departure point on the river, where you'll push off aboard your large raft and begin to lazily drift along the Deschutes, perhaps taking the opportunity to go for a swim. Before long, you'll need to climb back into the raft in anticipation of the now approaching Big Eddy rapid. Pay attention to your guide, and get ready to paddle, paddle, paddle! Your hearts will race, water will splash, someone will fall *into* the raft on the big drop...and you'll all want to do it again and again!

- Morning and afternoon departures 7 days a week from Bend and Sunriver.
- 1.25 Hours on the water covering 3 river miles.
- Appropriate for kids 6 and older.
- Up to 7 guests per raft.
- Includes transportation, professional-grade equipment, splash gear if needed, and expert interpretive guiding.

From Sun Country's web site...

- You will get wet. Really wet. So don't wear your nice shoes or clothes. A swimsuit and sandals (not flip flops) are great.
- Remember to bring and use sunscreen.
- Kids 6 and older will have an absolute blast.
- Don't show up drunk or with beer. This is not a lazy river float.
- Be cool and tip your guide.

Sun Country Tours
531 SW 13 Street
Bend, OR 97702
541-382-1709

Sun Country Tours
57100 Beaver Drive - Bldg. 26
Sunriver, OR 97707
541-382-1709

Explore Bend: Tumalo Falls

Falling nearly 100 feet from a wide notch, Tumalo Falls rewards visitors with a view of its picturesque drop only minutes from the parking area. However, don't be fooled into thinking that's all there is, as the trail winds its way up to the crest of the falls before continuing on through the forest for approximately four miles past numerous smaller falls on Tumalo Creek before arriving at Happy Valley.

Note: Tumalo Falls is not located at Tumalo State Park, but instead approximately 14 miles west of Bend at the very end of Skyliners Road. (See directions on the next page) A NW Forest Pass is required to park here. If you do not have a parking pass, you may purchase a daily parking pass with a credit card at a small kiosk located on your right *approximately ½ mile before arriving at the trailhead.* Stop here, buy your pass, *and then* proceed to a parking spot. Note that parking is not allowed on the north side of the road.

Explore Bend: Bridge Creek Falls at Tumalo Falls

For us, the main attraction of the Bridge Creek Falls trail isn't the beautiful 25' Bridge Creek Falls, which can be (partially) viewed from two viewpoints located a little less than a mile up the trail, but instead the pristine and undisturbed forest through which the trail traverses, beginning as you approach the one mile point.

Located within the municipal watershed for Bend, the trail navigates a forest floor that has seen fire and wind, but no logging. As a result, the understory isn't clear of debris, like you see as you drive up Skyliners, but is instead littered with the logs and other deadfall of an old forest. It looks almost "cluttered", but this is actually the more natural state of a forest, and it makes for a unique hike.

Bridge Creek is a tributary of Tumalo Creek, and as such its trailhead is the same as the Tumalo Falls trailhead. Park as you would for Tumalo Falls, and find the Bridge Creek Falls Trail breaking west off of the Tumalo Falls trail only a short distance up from the trailhead, after the cyclone fence ends. Note that this is a day use only trail, and no dogs or bikes are allowed.

Driving Directions: Follow Skyliners Road west out of Bend for 11 plus miles and cross a small bridge over Tumalo Creek, where the pavement ends. Veer left here and pass through a road gate, continuing for 2.5 miles to the Tumalo Falls trailhead. A Northwest Forest Pass or $5.00 daily permit is required to park here, and a daily permit may be purchased with a credit card at a small kiosk *located on your right approximately ½ mile before arriving at the trailhead.* Note that the road gate closes during the winter season.

BEND **Explore Bend:** High Desert Museum

The world of Oregon's High Desert and its unique cultural history come alive in the abundance of impressive exhibits and displays found throughout the High Desert Museum. Step inside to visit an authentic homestead from 1904, learn about the fascinating culture of the Native Americans who lived throughout Central Oregon, listen as a historic character shares with you about the daily lives of the early explorers and settlers who came to the area, see a turn-of-the-19th century sawmill and more before continuing outside to get close up views of the area's native wildlife, including birds of prey, river otters, and even porcupines!

High Desert Museum
59800 US Hwy 97
Bend, OR 97702
541-382-4754

Explore Bend: Bessie Butte

It's always great to find a short hike with a (relatively) low amount of effort that pays off with a big reward. The Bessie Butte trail is such a hike. Rising 500' above the surrounding terrain, the wide open "summit" of Bessie Butte provides a perfect spot for watching a sunset or a moonrise, all while looking out over all of Central Oregon with the Three Sisters, Mt. Bachelor, Mt. Hood, Smith Rock, and much more set out in the distance.

Rated: Moderate. Hike 1.5 miles on a moderately steep trail to the summit where you'll find a couple of simple wooden benches. We think the best view is in the southwest portion of the summit area. Dogs are allowed. Dress appropriately, as the trail and summit are somewhat exposed.

Directions: From Bend, drive south on Hwy 97 and take Exit 143 for Baker Rd. / Knott Rd. Turn left and follow Knott Rd. for 1.4 miles to China Hat Road, where you'll turn right and continue for another 4.6 miles to a road leading off to the right. Follow this for 1/3 mile to the obvious parking area and trailhead for Bessie Butte.

CYCLING BEND

Bend is the place to be if you're planning on riding bikes, be it catching air on a mountain bike trail, putting in 50 miles on a road bike up to Mt. Bachelor and back, exploring a new gravel route, or simply taking a leisurely ride along the river through the cool shade of towering Ponderosa pines.

There are *countless* routes in and around Bend, as well as throughout Central Oregon, and we have included a sample of some classic Bend casual rides here as an introduction. Pick up a copy of our book, *Central Oregon - An Explorer's Guide* for additional road rides and MTB trails, or visit the following web sites for more route descriptions and information...

- www.RideOregonRide.com
- http://cotamtb.com/trails/
- http://www.visitbend.com/Bend_Oregon_Activities_Recreation/Summer-Fun/Biking/Mountain-Biking/

Bike Rentals

You didn't bring a bike to Bend, but you want to ride? No worries, since there are quite a few shops in town that can set you up with a road, gravel, or mountain bike rental.

Here are three bike shops to get you started...

Pine Mountain Sports

Stocked with all kinds of great outdoor gear, be it for skiing, hiking, or cycling, Pine Mountain Sports is ready to get you set to experience the Bend outdoors. They can even adjust or fix your current ride to get you back on the trail...or road...or snow...

Pine Mountain Sports
255 SW Century Drive
Bend, OR 97702
541-385-8080

- Open: Monday through Friday - 10:00 a.m. - 6:00 p.m., Saturday and Sunday: 9:00 a.m. - 6:00 p.m.

Hutch's Bicycles

With two locations in Bend, Hutch's does cycling, and they do it well. Stop in to see the newest rides, pick up some gear, or rent a bike for the day, weekend, or longer. They will get you out and onto some new terrain in no time.

Hutch's Bicycles
725 NW Columbia St.
Bend, OR 97703
541-382-9253

Hutch's Bicycles
820 NE 3rd Street
Bend, OR 97701
541-382-6248

- Open: Monday - Saturday: 10:00 a.m. to 6:00 p.m., Sunday: 10:00 a.m. to 5:00 p.m.

WebCyclery

Can't choose between cycling or skiing? Don't worry, because WebCyclery handles both. Stop by to rent a road, gravel, mountain, or city bike and to get some beta on the best routes and current road and trail conditions.

WebCyclery & WebSkis
157 NW Franklin Ave.
Bend, OR 97703
541-318-6188

- Open: Monday - Friday - 9:00 a.m. to 6:00 p.m., Saturday - 9:00 a.m. to 5:00 p.m., Closed on Sunday.

Casual Riding

If you'd like to enjoy a casual ride along a flat paved or dirt road, perhaps to an interpretive center or a cool ice cream cone with your name on it, then the following collection of rides is just what you're looking for.

Note that an annual NW Forest Pass or $5.00 Day pass is required to park wherever a "Recreation Fee Required" sign is posted, including at the trailheads of the rides which appear on the following pages. These include Lava Island, Big Eddy, Aspen, Dillon Falls, Slough, and Benham Falls. Day passes may be purchased at the kiosk immediately to the left when turning onto FS Rd. 41 from the Cascade Lakes Scenic Byway / Century Drive, and NW Forest Passes may be purchased at a number of locations in Bend and the surrounding area, including the Cascade Lakes Welcome Station across from the entrance to FS Rd. 41, Pine Mountain Sports, Powder House, Sunnyside Sports and elsewhere.

Casual Riding: Cascade Lakes Welcome Station Ride - On the Rim Rock Trail

Set out on a pleasant and easy 5.4 mile roundtrip ride along a paved path that winds its way through the forest to the Cascade Lakes Welcome Station - Ranger Station along Century Drive / Cascade Lakes National Scenic Byway.

Driving Directions: Park at the Rimrock Trailhead parking area a short distance west of Bend on the Cascade Lakes National Scenic Byway / Century Drive and follow the paved pathway that leads through the tunnel under Century Drive for 2.7 miles as it leads west to the Cascade Lakes Welcome Station. Here, you'll find some interpretive information, a shady rest area, and a drinking fountain. A parking permit is not required.

Rimrock Trailhead
18775 Cascade Lakes National Scenic Byway
Bend, OR 97702

Note that the Rimrock Trailhead and the nearby forested off-leash Good Dog! area are popular with dog owners.

Casual Riding: Benham Falls to The Lava Lands Visitor Center & Lava Butte

Offering a smooth paved path through the forest, this 4.5 mile ride (9 miles roundtrip) takes you from Benham Falls to Lava Butte and the Lava Lands Visitor Center, all on a steady slight grade with no cars. Once at the visitor center, enjoy its interpretive displays before hiking the paved "Trail of the Molten Land" through an amazing lunar-like landscape of jagged A'a lava to a viewpoint at the base of Lava Butte, where you can admire a vast lava field spread out beneath an amazing view of the Oregon Cascades. In addition to the visitor center and a couple of short interpretive hikes, you'll find a shuttle runs from the visitor center to the 5,020' summit of Lava Butte approximately every 20 minutes during late May through early September. The fee to ride the shuttle is $2.00, *and exact change is required.* At the summit, you can visit the working fire lookout and gaze out over all of Central Oregon.

Note that the Black Rock Trail will also take you to the Lava Lands Visitor Center. It's a 4.5 mile casual dirt singletrack, which, while off in the forest, parallels the paved trail and begins on your left shortly after crossing the railroad tracks.

Driving Directions: Leave Bend and follow Century Drive / The Mt. Bachelor Highway west until a little bit after The Inn of the Seventh Mountain, where you will take a *left* onto Forest Service Road 41. (You'll see a large sign for this on the right which reads *Deschutes River Rec. Sites*) Follow FS Rd. 41 for four miles until you see the sign for the turnoff to Benham Falls. Turn left here and take this gravel road for 2.2 miles to the parking area. Unload your bikes and follow the flat dirt road that leads beyond the restroom and information kiosk/trailhead sign. This soon crosses a bridge over the Deschutes River before continuing on a wide paved path. Look for a directional sign to the Lava Lands Visitor Center shortly after crossing the bridge and climbing a short hill. Note that shortly after you turn east toward the Lava Lands Visitor Center, you will pop out onto a wide paved road. Ride east on this road, cross the railroad tracks and look for the paved trail to begin again on your left. This is also where you will pick up the Black Rock singletrack trail, if you choose.

Casual Riding: Benham Falls to Sunriver Resort

This paved bike route is the same as the Benham Falls to Lava Lands Visitor Center ride on the previous page, but instead of turning left/east toward the visitor center, you continue straight south to Sunriver Resort.

Driving Directions: Leave Bend and follow Century Drive / The Mt. Bachelor Highway west until a little bit after The Inn of the Seventh Mountain, where you will take a *left* onto Forest Service Road 41. (You'll see a large sign for this on the right which reads *Deschutes River Rec. Sites.*) Follow FS Rd. 41 for four miles until you see the sign for the turnoff to Benham Falls. Turn left here and take this gravel road for 2.2 miles to the parking area. Unload your bikes and follow the flat dirt road that leads beyond the restroom and information kiosk/trailhead sign. This soon crosses a bridge over the Deschutes River before continuing on a wide paved path to the northern end of the bike trails of Sunriver Resort.

Note: The bike trails of Sunriver Resort can be confusing, so it would be good to familiarize yourself with the trails online before going. If you feel ambitious, you can ride all the way south to the Sunriver shopping area, where you'll find handy maps...as well as ice cream, shopping, restaurants and the large and active SHARC water park.

Casual Riding: Lava Island Falls to Benham Falls - Continue to Sunriver

This is an excellent and fairly casual mountain biking trail that primarily follows an old road through beautiful forest stands along the Deschutes River, though some of it is also on single-track.

Approximately 7 miles from Lava Island Falls to Benham Falls. Note that there are some very scenic viewpoints of the Deschutes River along the way.

Driving Directions: Leave Bend and follow Century Drive / the Mt. Bachelor Highway west until shortly after The Inn of the Seventh Mountain, where you will take a *left* onto Forest Service Road 41. (You'll see a large sign for this on the right which reads *Deschutes River Rec. Sites.*) Follow FS Rd. 41 for approximately 1/8 mile until you see the sign for Lava Island Falls on the left. (FS Road 4100 / 800) Take this gravel road and park in the parking area. Find the bike trail, *not the hiking trail right next to the river*, and follow it south / upriver to Dillon Falls, The Slough, Benham Falls and, if you choose, Sunriver Resort via the route description on the previous page.

Note: It is possible to temporarily lose this trail when you cross the roads leading to some of the main parking areas providing access to the Deschutes River, such as Dillon Falls, the Slough, etc. In most cases, if the trail is not readily apparent on the opposite side of the road you've reached, then head left and follow the road a short distance until you find the trail again.

Note: If you ever find yourself leaving a parking area and switchbacking down a trail toward the river, (Near the Aspen Trailhead) then you're off route. Go back to the parking area and find the *broad road*, which is behind a large gate, and follow this.

This trail travels south from the Lava Island Falls parking area and crosses the parking areas for Aspen, Dillon Falls, The Slough and Benham Falls as it travels along the Deschutes River. If you'd like to shorten this bike trip, then continue on Forest Service Rd. 41 until you see one of the roads leading to any of these trailheads, then take it, park and leave from there.

Important: This bike trail parallels a hiking trail. For the most part, these two trails do not interconnect, except once you get to The Slough parking area. At this point, you will ride on the hiking trail from The Slough to Benham Falls, so slow your speed and keep an eye out for hikers. Once at Benham Falls, you'll get back onto the very obvious dirt road, (closed to cars) which continues south from the parking area.

Forest Service Road 41 & Upper Deschutes River Recreation Area

East of Bend, just off of the Cascade Lakes Scenic Byway / Century Drive, is Forest Service Road 41. Leading into the Upper Deschutes River Recreation Area, FS Rd. 41 provides access to popular hiking and biking trails, up close waterfall views, whitewater rafting and kayaking spots, fishing holes, and more, all along scenic stretches of the Deschutes River. In addition to what you find on the following pages, be sure to look at the Casual Bicycle Rides found off of FS Rd. 41, which are found on page 52.

Parking Passes

Note that an annual NW Forest Pass or $5.00 Day pass is required to park wherever a "Recreation Fee Required" sign is posted in the FS Rd. 41 area, which includes the trailheads at Lava Island, Big Eddy, Aspen, Dillon Falls, Slough, and Benham Falls. Day passes may be purchased at the kiosk immediately to the left when turning onto FS Rd. 41 from the Cascade Lakes Scenic Byway / Century Drive, and annual NW Forest Passes may be purchased at a number of locations in the area, including the Cascade Lakes Welcome Station across from the entrance to FS Rd. 41, Pine Mountain Sports, Powder House, Sunnyside Sports, South Twin Resort, Crane Prairie Resort, Cultus Lake Resort, and elsewhere.

The following pages reflect four scenic sections of the Deschutes River Trail winding their way from Lava Island Falls upriver to Big Eddy, then Big Eddy to Aspen, followed by Aspen to Dillon Falls, and then finishing with Dillon Falls to Benham Falls. You will find trailheads at the beginning of each section, and you can combine any or all four sections for a great hike year-round, which are as enjoyable heading upriver as they are down.

Forest Service Road 41: Deschutes River Trail - Lava Island Falls to Big Eddy

The northern most trailhead, and the first one you come to off of FS 41, is Lava Island Falls. Head downriver, and you'll reach the Meadow Picnic Trailhead, but if you hike upriver for one mile through a shady forest of Ponderosa Pines next to the river, you'll come to Big Eddy. All during the warm summer months, rafters pull out at Big Eddy and then walk a little ways downstream to scope the major rapids they're about to drift through. Somewhat concerned, and oftentimes terrified, they then climb back into their rafts, bounce their way through the rapids with a skilled river guide at the stern, and then wish they could do it all over again right away! You can watch the rafters up close by sitting on one of the boulders at the river's edge, right by the frothing rapids. Look for the boulders and rafters when you begin to see split rail fences along the trail. This is also a great spot to have some lunch.

Note: A Northwest Forest Pass is required for parking at the Lava Island Falls trailhead. As an alternative, you may pay the $5.00 day use fee. See the previous page for more details.

Driving Directions: Drive west on Century Drive toward Mt. Bachelor. Shortly after passing The Inn of the Seventh Mountain, you'll turn south onto Forest Service Road 41. (You'll see a big sign for this on the right which reads *Deschutes River Rec. Sites.*) Follow this until you see the small sign for Lava Island Falls. Turn left onto this gravel road and proceed to the trailhead.

Forest Service Road 41: Deschutes River Trail - Big Eddy to Aspen

Like the Lava Island Falls to Big Eddy section of the Deschutes River Trail, the next leg upriver, the Big Eddy to Aspen section, makes its way through a Ponderosa Pine forest along a scenic section of the Deschutes for one mile to the Aspen trailhead.

Driving Directions: Drive west on Century Drive toward Mt. Bachelor. Shortly after passing The Inn of the Seventh Mountain, you'll turn south onto Forest Service Road 41. (You'll see a big sign for this on the right which reads *Deschutes River Rec. Sites.*) Follow this until you see the small sign for Big Eddy / Aspen. Turn left onto this gravel road and at the upcoming "T" turn left to proceed to the trailhead.

Forest Service Road 41: Deschutes River Trail - Aspen to Dillon Falls

"It's the same, but different." Of the different trail sections along the Deschutes River in this area, in our opinion the section from Aspen to Dillon Falls offers the most character. Leave the parking area and take the long switchback down to the trailhead found near the boat ramp. From here, you'll hike through a grove of aspens next to a serene green meadow bordering the river. The meadow continues along the river, at times inviting you to walk through it to stand alongside the Deschutes where you'll see beautiful scenery, a variety of birds, and if you're lucky, a river otter making its way along the far bank. Continue to the one mile point where you'll begin to hear and see the rapids at the tail end of Dillon Falls. From here, climb a steep section of log and trail stairs before proceeding a short distance to Dillon Falls. Note that this makes for a very nice hike during the morning or evening hours. 1.4 Miles from Aspen to Dillon Falls.

Driving Directions: Drive west on Century Drive toward Mt. Bachelor. Shortly after passing The Inn of the Seventh Mountain, you'll turn south onto Forest Service Road 41. (You'll see a big sign for this on the right which reads *Deschutes River Rec. Sites.*) Follow this until you see the small sign for Big Eddy / Aspen. Turn left onto this gravel road and at the upcoming "T" turn right to proceed to the trailhead.

Forest Service Road 41: Dillon Falls

A short 1/8 mile hike downriver from the parking area brings you to Dillon Falls. Here, the calm Deschutes picks up speed before suddenly dropping 15' into a large pool, where it churns violently before flowing out into class-5 whitewater.

Note: A Northwest Forest Pass is required for parking at Dillon Falls. As an alternative, you may pay the $5.00 day use fee.

Driving Directions: Drive west on Century Drive toward Mt. Bachelor. Shortly after passing The Inn of the Seventh Mountain, you'll turn south onto Forest Service Road 41.

(You'll see a big sign for this on the right which reads *Deschutes River Rec. Sites.*) Follow this until you see the small sign for Dillon Falls. Turn left onto this gravel road and park in the parking area for the falls, not the kayak launching area next to the water, and then hike a short distance *downriver* to Dillon Falls.

Forest Service Road 41: Deschutes River Trail - Dillon Falls to Benham Falls

This is a nice hike showcasing the beauty of the Deschutes River as it winds its way from one set of falls to another before the trail leads you back to your car. Begin by making your way upriver as you hike between the Deschutes and a large quiet meadow before entering a forest of pines where the trail continues to climb and fall as the river flows below, at times peaceful and at others as rushing whitewater, all before reaching an overlook at turbulent Benham Falls.

Driving Directions: Drive west on Century Drive toward Mt. Bachelor. Shortly after passing The Inn of the Seventh Mountain, you'll turn south onto Forest Service Road 41. (You'll see a big sign for this on the right which reads *Deschutes River Rec. Sites.*) Follow this until you see the small sign for Dillon Falls. Turn left onto this gravel road and continue to the trailhead, parking in the parking area for the falls, not the kayak launching area next to the water. Then hike a short 1/8 mile *downriver* to see Dillon Falls before turning around and hiking *upriver* for 3.2 miles to Benham Falls. Return the way you came for 6.4 miles roundtrip.

Note: A Northwest Forest Pass is required for parking at Dillon Falls. As an alternative, you may pay the $5.00 day use fee. Passes are available at the Cascade Lakes Welcome Station, located across from the entrance to FS Road 41.

Forest Service Road 41: Benham Falls

A short hike of a couple hundred yards takes you from the parking area to an overlook for Benham Falls, which dramatically tumbles and froths its way through a narrow passage directly in front of the viewpoint. This is an impressive waterfall anytime of the year, particularly during the spring and winter months when the water volume increases or the temperature drops below freezing.

Note: Keep an eye out for kayakers, who will sometimes navigate the falls when the water volume increases. To see the falls from above, take the broad dirt road/trail that leads beyond the restroom in the parking area and after a short distance look for a smaller trail on the left that leads down to the river.

Note: A Northwest Forest Pass is required for parking here. As an alternative, you may pay the $5.00 day use fee.

Driving Directions: Leave Bend and follow Century Drive / The Mt. Bachelor Highway west until a little bit after The Inn of the Seventh Mountain, where you will take a *left* onto Forest Service Road 41. (You'll see a large sign for this on the right which reads *Deschutes River Rec. Sites.*) Follow FS Rd. 41 for four miles until you see the sign for the turnoff to Benham Falls. Turn left here and take this gravel road for 2.2 miles to the parking area.

Tonight's Lodging - McMenamins Old St. Francis School

Your first two nights lodging on your Southeast Oregon road trip isn't so much historical as it is "old school"...literally. Built in 1936 as a large brick Catholic schoolhouse, McMenamins Old St. Francis School in old town Bend welcomes visitors with classrooms that have been converted into 60 different guest rooms. In addition, you can wander its long hallways to find a pub, brewery, restaurant, live music, outdoor patios, a soaking pool, and more. Be sure to check

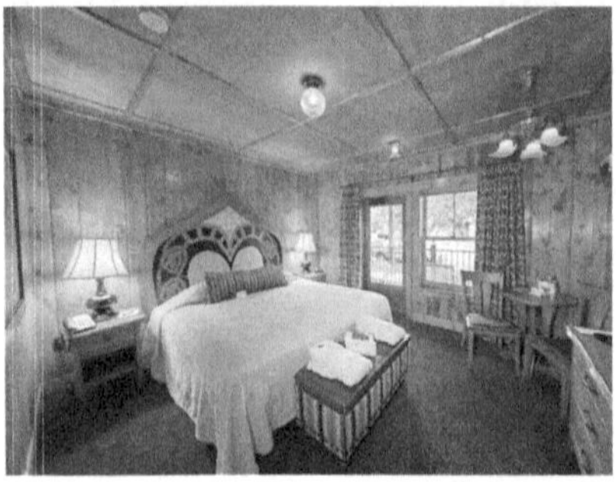

what time the movie begins, as the Old St. Francis School also contains a theatre where you can watch first or second run movies while enjoying dinner and a handcrafted McMenamins ale or a glass of wine, all from a comfy oversized chair or sofa. Oh, and popcorn, too.

McMenamins Old St. Francis School
700 NW Bond Street
Bend, OR 97703
541-382-5174

Important!

Note that you'll begin your road trip by making a reservation at McMenamins in Bend for your first two nights. At the end of your journey, you can choose to finish back in Bend, instead of going home. If you'd like to remain in Bend for a few more days and nights after your road trip to explore Bend's many adventures and activities, you may want to make reservations for those nights now, as well.

Lodging Options

Bend offers visitors an abundance of lodging options, though most are not historic. We recommend you consider one of these choices:

- Mt. Bachelor Village Resort
- Seventh Mountain Resort
- The Oxford Hotel
- Pine Ridge Inn
- Numerous Name Brand Hotels
- Numerous Vacation Rentals

In addition, an online search of lodging choices available in Bend will return many, many options to choose from.

DAY THREE

BEND TO PRAIRIE CITY

Metasequoia - Dawn Redwood
Oregon State Fossil

Day 3
Bend to Prairie City

Day 3 – Date: / /

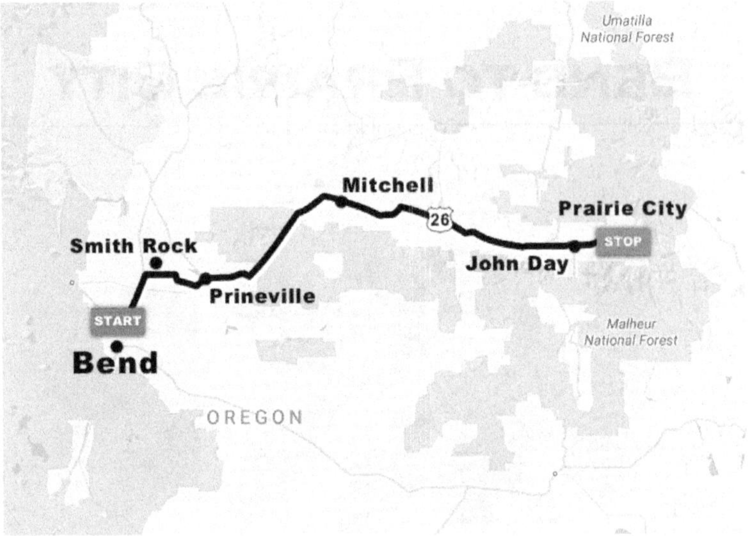

Summary: Where You're Going Today

- Smith Rock State Park
- Prineville, OR
- The Painted Hills
- Mitchell, OR
- Dayville, OR
- Prairie City, OR

The third day of your road trip introduces you to the geological and scenic wonders of the area known as the "Oregon Frontier". Here, you venture out into eastern Central Oregon, where you'll be amazed at the awe inspiring world of Smith Rock State Park, home to soaring stone walls and world class rock climbing, before making your way toward

Prineville and then Mitchell, the gateway to the colorful and one-of-a-kind Painted Hills. From there, you'll continue eastward to the quiet town of Prairie City, where you'll stay for the night.

Be sure to grab your rock hammer, field notebook and magnifying glass, as you'll be exploring all the way through the Oligocene, Cenozoic, Cretaceous, Paleogene, Neogene, and Quarternary periods of the John Day Fossil Beds!

Tonight's Lodging:

- Historic Hotel Prairie

Today's Mileage: 215 Miles

Reservations Needed for This Segment:

- Historic Hotel Prairie - 541-820-4800

Before You Leave:

Fill your gas tank in Bend, Redmond, Terrebonne, or Prineville. Gas is also available today in Mitchell, Dayville, Mt. Vernon, John Day, and Prairie City. By the way, this small gas pump icon, which you'll see throughout the book, is the actual gas pump you'll soon see in Frenchglen, Oregon.

Start

You'll leave Bend today and drive north on Hwy 97 to the small town of Terrebonne and the stunning geological wonder that is Smith Rock State Park.

Terrebonne Stop: Crescent Moon Ranch

Known around the world for its prize-winning alpacas, but located here, right next to Hwy 97 on the south end of Terrebonne, the Crescent Moon Ranch is home to hundreds of furry alpacas of all sizes and colors. Stop in to feed and pet the alpacas, perhaps see some cute babies, and shop in the small boutique filled with high-quality alpaca fur products.

Crescent Moon Ranch
7566 US-97
Terrebonne, OR 97760

- Open Daily - 10:00 a.m. - 4:00 p.m.

Driving Directions: Drive north on Hwy 97 from Bend for approximately 30 minutes, and you'll see the Crescent Moon Ranch on your right just as you approach town.

Smith Rock State Park

Located 26 miles (45 Minutes) north of Bend, just east of Terrebonne, OR, Smith Rock State Park is one of Oregon's most impressive and picturesque parks. With its soaring walls and dramatic volcanic features, world-class rock climbing, miles of hiking and mountain biking trails, sublime views, and an abundance of wildlife, all accented by the tranquilly flowing Crooked River, it makes for a day of casual or full-on world class adventure.

Depending upon the activities you've chosen to explore along your road trip route today, you may wish to enjoy the captivating view from the rim overlooking the park, or hike down to the dihedrals area via the 2.5 mile *River Trail to The Dihedrals* to watch world class rock climbing up close. If you decide to do the hike, be sure to pick up one of the free 2" x 5" Smith Rock pocket maps at a parking lot kiosk or the Welcome Center yurt before exploring the park.

Visit the Welcome Center Yurt and Overlook Rim

If hiking doesn't fit your schedule today, then simply visit the Welcome Center Yurt in the middle of the parking area and step inside to see its interpretive displays, which explain all about the geology, flora, fauna, rock climbing and history of Smith Rock State Park. Afterwards, make your way to the expansive viewing area at the rim overlooking the park to take in the impressive views.

River Trail to The Dihedrals - 2.5 Miles Roundtrip

The most popular trail at Smith Rock, the River Trail takes hikers along the Crooked River to some of the best scenic locations found within the park. From the Welcome Center Yurt, hike north a short distance via the main trail to the viewpoint overlooking the main Smith Rock formation and drop down the steep Chute Trail or the lesser grade Canyon Trail to the bridge crossing the Crooked River below. After crossing the bridge, hike west along the River Trail to The Dihedrals area, which is likely to be busy with rock climbers testing their skills on an abundance of routes. Watch them from the River Trail or hike up to the base of the routes for a closer vantage point. Note that this can be a long 2.5 miles roundtrip in the hot summer sun, so be sure to use sunscreen and bring plenty of water.

Driving Directions to Smith Rock State Park

Drive north from Bend for 30 minutes on Hwy 97 to Terrebonne and then turn east onto Smith Rock Way. Follow the signs to the park, which is plainly visible from Terrebonne.

Parking at Smith Rock

Note that an annual or daily Oregon State Park parking permit is required when parking at Smith Rock. Permits are available for purchase at the Welcome Center yurt, as well as at automated kiosks in the different parking areas.

PRINEVILLE, OR

While some Central Oregon towns suddenly sprang to life with the call of "Gold!" from the waters of a nearby stream, Prineville's rich history began with the call of "Timber!" from deep within what is today the Ochoco National Forest. Realizing its potential, the town voted to build the first municipally run railroad in the country, the City of Prineville Railroad, to extract timber and bring it to the city's mills, thus creating a period of prosperity that lasted for decades. Today, the past moves toward the future with Prineville now being the home to large data centers run by the likes of Apple and Facebook / Meta.

Prineville Stop: A. R. Bowman Museum

Housed in the 1910 Crook County Bank Building built of heavy stone, the A. R. Bowman Museum reveals the history of Crook County and Central Oregon. Its two floors showcase the items used in the daily lives of pioneers, the tools of the ranching and timber industry, life on the City of Prineville Railroad, and a wealth of historic photos complementing over 700 reference books on Oregon history.

A. R. Bowman Museum
246 North Main Street
Prineville, OR 97754
541-447-3715

- Monday - Friday: 10:00 a.m. - 5:00 p.m.
- Saturday & Sunday: 11:00 a.m. - 4:00 p.m.

Prineville Stop: Tastee Treet

If the timing is right, consider having lunch at the Tastee Treet. A Prineville icon for over 60 years, this small old-school diner offers a large selection of menu items, including hearty burgers made with local beef and served with hand-cut fries. Top it off with a cool drink, a shake, or even an ice cream cone, and you're good to go.

Tastee Treet
493 NE 3rd Street
Prineville, OR 97754

- Open: Daily - 5:00 a.m. to 8:00 p.m.
- Serves Breakfast, Lunch & Dinner.
- Many gluten free options are available

Prineville Stop: Steins Pillar

Towering above a forest of Ponderosa Pine trees in the Ochoco mountains east of Prineville is Steins Pillar, a 350' high rock monolith standing like a skyscraper made of stone. In case you're wondering, yes, rock climbers do climb it, and they do so by three different routes.

Directions to the Viewpoint: From the A. R. Bowman Museum on the corner of NE 3rd Street and N Main Street in Prineville, drive east on Hwy 26 for 9.3 miles to Mill Creek

Road. Turn left/north onto Mill Creek Road and follow this for 8 miles to a viewpoint for Steins Pillar. Note that there are a few turnouts along the way, each with a view of the pillar, but the "official" viewpoint has a large parking area with a wood railing fence and interpretive sign. *Photo courtesy of Chris Winter*

Hike to Steins Pillar

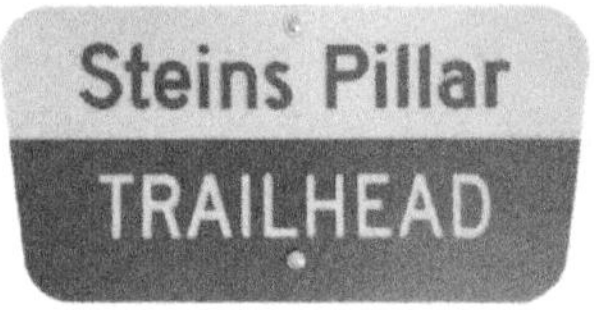

For a close up look at Steins Pillar, including from its base, hike the Steins Pillar trail. This moderate 4 mile roundtrip out and back trail leads you through a quiet ponderosa pine forest to a rocky viewpoint offering a captivating view of the pillar. If you'd like, you can continue down through a series of switchbacks to the pillar's base, where you just might see some rock climbers scaling its handful of routes to the summit.

Directions to the Trailhead: From the A. R. Bowman Museum on the corner of NE 3rd Street and N Main Street in Prineville, drive east on Hwy 26 for 9.3 miles to Mill Creek Road. Turn left/north onto Mill Creek Road and follow this for 6.7 miles to a road leading to the right, which will take you up to the Steins Pillar trailhead in 2 miles.

MITCHELL, OR

Mitchell Stop: The Painted Hills

Truly unlike anything or anywhere else in Oregon, the Painted Hills immerse visitors in a surreal landscape. What appears to be mountains in the distance are actually smaller hills nearby, their scale distorted by the effects of erosion and color. Here, entire hillsides of claystones are covered in layers of reds, yellows, golds, tans, greens, purples and more, all of them altering in color and intensity throughout each day, season and change of the weather. Late afternoons and early mornings provide lighting which adds to the richness of the color and beauty of the area.

Visitors will find a raised boardwalk winding through the hills, along with four short hikes and a picnic area. We recommend the Painted Hills Overlook Trail (1/2 Mile round-trip) to give you an excellent overview of the area. Located 9 miles northwest of Mitchell, Oregon.

The Painted Hills
37375 Bear Creek Rd.
Mitchell, OR 97750

Driving Directions: While traveling east toward Mitchell, OR on Hwy 26, you'll see a large sign for the turnoff to The Painted Hills approximately 3.5 miles *before* reaching Mitchell. Turn left / north here onto Burnt Ranch Road and follow this for 6 miles to the parking area for The Painted Hills.

Mitchell Stop: Mitchell, OR

Founded in 1873, Mitchell, Oregon is known as the gateway to the Painted Hills. "A diamond in the rough with big potential", Mitchell welcomes visitors with a bit of an unsettled exterior, which is quickly changing.

In addition to a general store, there are a handful of restaurants in Mitchell, such as the quaint Bridge Creek Café, Painted Hills Pastry, and Tiger Town Brewing Company. Take a moment to walk the town, explore Judy's Place for some antiques, stop in at the historic Oregon Hotel, and check out the Spoke'n Hostel just west of town, "an oasis and respite for bicycle tourists traveling the Trans America Trail between John Day and Prineville, Oregon." (541-462-3333) Note that road trippers traveling by car are more than welcome to stay here, as well.

Bridge Creek Café
218 US-26
Mitchell, OR 97750
541-777-7132

Spoke'n Hostel
300 US-26
Mitchell, OR 97750
541-462-3333

Driving Directions: From the Painted Hills, return south to Hwy 26 and turn left / east. You'll reach Mitchell in 3.5 miles.

JOHN DAY FOSSIL BEDS NATIONAL MONUMENT

The John Day Fossil Beds National Monument is comprised of three large "units" encompassing nearly 14,000 acres. These include The Clarno Unit, which is west of Fossil, OR, the Painted Hills Unit, found northwest of Mitchell, OR, and the Sheep Rock Unit, which is bisected by the Journey Through Time Scenic Byway / Hwy 19. Each unit consists of captivating geologic formations home to an abundance of animal and plant fossils telling the ever emerging story of Oregon's ancient ecosystems spanning over 40 million years. The headquarters of the National Monument is the Thomas Condon Paleontology and Visitor Center, which showcases the treasures found throughout these three units with a collection of interesting exhibits and a working lab.

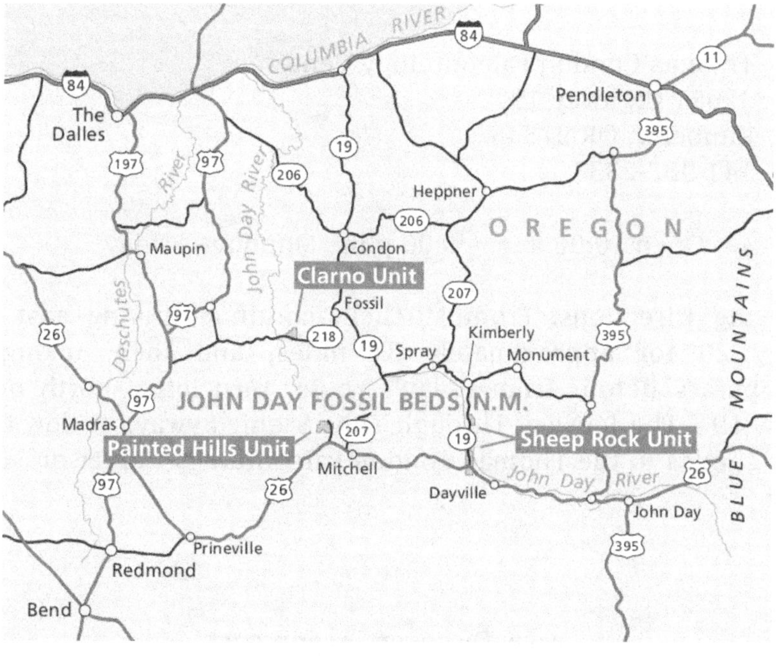

Next Stop: Thomas Condon Paleontology Center

As you make your way through the John Day Fossil Beds National Monument you'll pass through three distinct "units"; The Clarno Unit, Sheep Rock, and the Painted Hills. The central research point for all three is the modern Thomas Condon Paleontology Center. Located opposite the majestic Sheep Rock, the center is home to numerous fascinating displays, a walk-through exhibit, touch tables, Junior Ranger programs, and a Fossil Laboratory where paleontologists study a collection of over 40,000 fossils. You're guaranteed to see fossils up close here!

Note: Be sure to pick up a free Oregon road map or buy a postcard and stamp it with a John Day Fossil Beds NM hand stamp, which you'll find by the entrance.

Thomas Condon Paleontology Center
32651 Highway 19
Kimberly, OR 97848
541-987-2333

- Open 10:00 a.m. - 5:00 p.m. Monday - Friday

Driving Directions: From Mitchell, continue driving east on Hwy 26 for approximately 31 miles, and then, taking a temporary detour from today's route, turn left / north onto Hwy 19 / The Journey Through Time Scenic Byway. Follow this for 2 miles to the Thomas Condon Paleontology Center on your left.

Next Stop: Cant Ranch House Museum

Built in 1917 by John and Elizabeth Cant, the stately Cant Ranch House Museum is a beautifully restored and maintained home which represents the history of agricultural farming, as well as sheep and cattle ranching, in the John Day area. Today it serves as part of the headquarters for the John Day Fossil Bed National Monument.

The museum itself is open to the public on limited occasions, but guests may stroll its scenic grounds, walk through the chicken coup, study the farm implements and sit in the shady apple and pear orchard while enjoying the view.

Cant Ranch House Museum
32651 Highway 19
Kimberly, OR 97848   (541-987-2333)

Driving Directions: Drive north on Hwy 19 for 0.1 mile to the Cant Ranch Museum on your right.

Next Stop: Dayville Mercantile

Stop in at "The Merc" to explore one of Oregon's oldest general stores, providing dry goods to locals since 1896, seventeen years before Dayville was founded. You'll also find a full-service bike shop for Trans America Trail riders and other cyclists.

Dayville Mercantile
207 Franklin St.
Dayville, OR 97825

Driving Directions: From the Cant Ranch House Museum, return south on Hwy 19 for 2.1 miles to the junction with Hwy 26. Turn left / east here and continue for 6.7 miles to the Dayville Mercantile on your left.

Next Stop: Dayville Cafe

If you're looking for a hearty country meal served by friendly folks, then you're looking for the family-owned Dayville Café. Stop in for lunch, and choose from a large selection of hearty burgers made with local beef, hand-cut fries, sandwiches, tacos, soups, salads, and other delicious menu items. Then complement it all with a milkshake, root beer float, lemonade, or tall refreshing soda. For dinner, tuck in your napkin and dine on wild caught salmon, cod, prawns, stuffed pork chops, chicken strips and juicy steaks. Save room, however, because you'll definitely want a slice from their selection of more than 40 homemade pies!

Call ahead to see if they are open today and if they're serving lunch or dinner, in addition to their regular breakfast offerings.

Dayville Café
212 Franklin Street
Dayville, OR 97825   (541-987-2122)

Driving Directions: The Dayville Café is located across the street from the Dayville Mercantile.

Next Stop: Prairie City, Oregon

It's time to wrap up your day and head to tonight's lodging in the small town of Prairie City. As you drive there, you'll pass through the town of John Day while heading east on Hwy 26. You'll be coming back this way, as John Day is your first stop tomorrow morning before heading south on Highway 395 toward Burns, OR.

Driving Directions: From Dayville, drive east on the Journey Through Time Scenic Byway / Hwy 26 for 44 miles to Prairie City, OR.

Note: As you travel to Prairie City, keep in mind that many of the restaurants in town close by 8:00 p.m. El Cocinero restaurant is often open until 9:00 p.m. - 541-820-4414

Tonight's Lodging - Historic Hotel Prairie Prairie City, OR

A highlight of your trip is a stay in the Historic Hotel Prairie. Built in 1910 to serve travelers to the area, as well as Sumpter Valley Railroad business clientele, this beautifully restored piece of Oregon history presents accommodations that "blend the charm of the past with the comfort of the present."

The Historic Hotel Prairie has nine rooms, including a spacious one-bedroom suite with a kitchen. All rooms include a private bath, offer cable TV and Wi-Fi, and are non-smoking.

Historic Hotel Prairie
112 Front Street
Prairie City, OR 97869
541-820-4800
HotelPrairie@ortelco.net

Lodging Option #1: Riverside School House B & B

Yes, this is a quaint B & B inside an old school house! Voted as one of the best places to stay in Oregon B & Bs, the historical Riverside School House is divided into two large suites, separated by French doors. The front suite has a queen and a double bed, bathroom and a small kitchen, while the rear suite has a small sitting room, a bedroom with a queen bed and a bathroom.

To ensure privacy, only one party may rent the school house at a time, whether you rent the front suite, rear suite or both.

Riverside School House B & B
28076 North River Road
Prairie City, OR 97869
541-820-4731
www.RiversideSchoolHouse.com

Note: The best way to make reservations or to receive information is via email at: RiversideRanchpcor@Gmail.com

Driving Directions: From the intersection of Hwy 26 and Main Street in Prairie City, drive south on South Main Street past the DeWitt Museum before turning left onto SW Bridge Street. Follow this as it turns into Summit Prairie Road/County Road 62 until you see a left turn for North River Road/County Road 61 (6.5 Miles from Prairie City) Turn left / west here and follow this ¼ mile to the Riverside School House B & B on the right.

Lodging Option #2: Pine Shadows Getaway

Located 10.5 miles southeast of Prairie City, Pine Shadows Getaway offers a small collection of luxurious cabins tucked under old growth Pines and Firs next to the headwaters of the John Day River. Inside each cabin, guests will find clean high-end amenities, including comfortable furniture, well-appointed kitchens, rain shower heads, lush towels, artisan soaps, and beds featuring down comforters and soft 600 thread count sheets. Outside, guests can fly fish, lie in a hammock, enjoy a spa, or sit around a fire ring while roasting marshmallows.

Pine Shadows Getaway Resort
25923 Green Haven Road
Prairie City, OR 97869
541-820-3736
PineShadowGetaway@gmail.com

- Open May 1st - October 1st.
- *Note: There is a 2 night minimum stay at the Pine Shadows Getaway, so if you choose to stay here, you'll need to add an additional day to your trip schedule.*

Driving Directions: From the intersection of Hwy 26 and Main Street in Prairie City, drive south on South Main Street past the DeWitt Museum before turning left onto SW Bridge Street. Follow this as it turns into Summit Prairie Road/County Road 62 for 10.5 miles until you see a sign on your left for Green Haven Rd. Turn left onto the gravel road, cross the river and Pine Shadows Getaway Resort will be the first gate on the left.

Notes

Day Four

Prairie City to Diamond

Day 4
Prairie City to Diamond

Day 4 – Date: / /

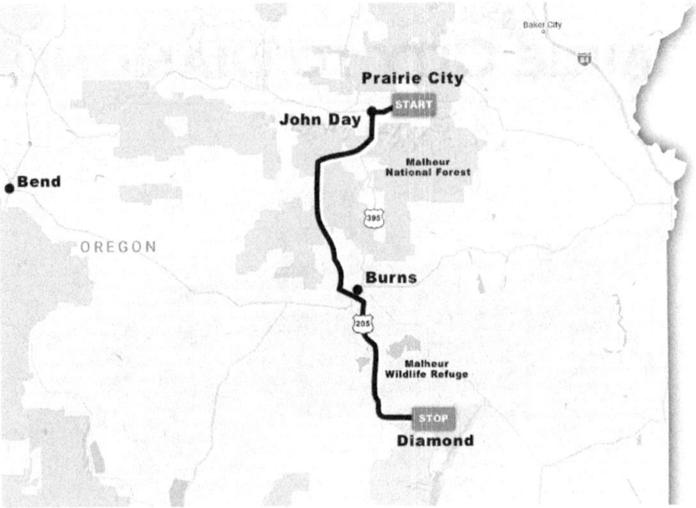

Summary: Where You're Going Today

- Prairie City, OR
- John Day, OR
- Canyon City, OR
- Burns, OR
- Malheur Wildlife Refuge
- Diamond, OR

With today's journey, you begin to head south, passing through the Malheur National Forest to begin your trek into the hay fields and wide open vistas of far southeast Oregon.

Tonight's Lodging:

- Historic Hotel Diamond

Gas is available today in Prairie City, John Day, Canyon City, and then not again until Burns. *You will want to fill or top off your tank in Burns.*

Today's Mileage: 160 Miles

Reservations Needed for This Segment:

- Historic Hotel Diamond - 541-493-1898
    - 1 Night's stay
    - Optional Dinner Reservations - 6:30 p.m.
    - Note: There are no other places to eat (or shop) in Diamond. If you are planning on dining at the Hotel Diamond at 6:30 p.m., be sure to plan your day accordingly. Groceries and dining are available in Burns, one hour north of Diamond.

- Kam Wah Chung State Heritage Site - 541-575-2800
    - Hours: 9:00 a.m. - Noon, 1:00 p.m. - 5:00 p.m.

Start

Start your day with a breakfast at Chuck's Little Diner, conveniently located a few doors down from the Historic Hotel Prairie on Main Street. Popular with locals, it serves ranch style breakfasts of fluffy pancakes, hash browns, bacon, sausage, homemade flaky biscuits, and eggs just the way you like them.

Chuck's Little Diner
Breakfast and Lunch
142 Front Street
Prairie City, OR 97869 (541-820-4353)

- Open 6:00 a.m. to 2:00 p.m.
- Closed Tuesdays and Wednesdays.

First Stop: DeWitt Museum Depot Park - Prairie City

Started in 1890, the Sumpter Valley Railway carried timber, mail, passengers and supplies along an 81-mile rail route between Baker City and Prairie City until 1947. Today, the DeWitt Museum is dedicated to preserving the history of this important rail line, showcasing artifacts from its everyday existence, including photographs of its massive locomotives and some of their spectacular wrecks, rare historical documents, railway antiques, tools, lanterns and more. In addition, the museum houses a large collection of various antiques, rocks and minerals gathered by the DeWitts as they traveled the world.

DeWitt Museum Depot Park
425 South Main St
Prairie City, Oregon 97869 (541-820-3330)

- Open 10:00 a.m. - 5:00 p.m., Wed. through Sat.
- Open May 15th through October 15th

Note: Sumpter Valley Railroad Restoration is doing some amazing work in restoring the Sumpter Valley Railway near Sumpter, Oregon, 44 miles to the northeast, off Hwy 7. Here you'll find powerful steam locomotives from the 1800s, restored rolling stock, new train depots and much more. Visit their web site at www.SumpterValleyRailroad.org. Note that a trip on the Sumpter Valley Railroad is part of our *Oregon Road Trips - Northeast Edition* book.

Driving Directions: From the Hotel Prairie, drive south on South Main Street for one third of a mile until you see the DeWitt Museum on your left.

JOHN DAY, OR

John Day, Oregon

The largest city in Grant County, historic John Day, Oregon is home to many unique shops, antique stores, restaurants, markets and more. We suggest you set aside time in your schedule to do some exploring, *especially of the Kam Wah Chung State Heritage Site.*

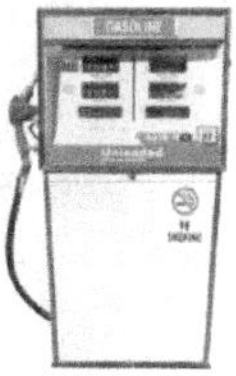

Note: Your next available gas is in Canyon City, which is just south of John Day, or in Burns, OR.

John Day Stop: John Day Farmers Market

Operating from the third Saturday in June to the third Saturday in October, the John Day Farmers Market offers a bounty of homemade and handmade goods, including locally harvested fruits and vegetables, fresh baked breads, confections, locally crafted jewelry, toys and other treasures you're sure to enjoy.

John Day Farmers Market
Across from The Outpost Pizza Pub & Grill
SW Brent Drive
John Day, OR 97845
831-596-0656

Driving Directions: Drive 13 miles *west* from Prairie City on the Journey Through Time Scenic Byway / Hwy 26 to John Day and find the Farmers Market lining each side of SW Brent Drive, opposite Outpost Pizza Pub & Grill and just after passing Canyon Blvd / Hwy 395.

John Day Stop: Kam Wah Chung State Heritage Site

A "must stop" on your Central Oregon road trip.

Built in the 1870s, a small non-descript building in John Day became home to Kam Wah Chung & Co. Here, two Chinese proprietors, Lung On and Ing "Doc" Hay, conducted business with the Chinese community of Eastern Oregon for more than 50 years, with Lung On running a general store, Post Office and library, and "Doc" Hay practicing Chinese medicine, with a focus on Pulsology, the diagnosing of ailments through the reading of one's pulse. In time, the two proprietors passed away, and in 1955 the building was closed. Its contents remained largely intact and preserved for 20 years, when it was reopened and restored as one of the most well preserved representations of the cultural, medicinal and pioneer life of Chinese immigrants in the early 20th century. Today, it is an Oregon State Park and National Historic Landmark.

We *highly* recommend you tour this fascinating historical museum, as well as visit the nearby Kam Wah Chung Interpretive Center.

- Museum tours operate daily May 1st to October 31st
- 9:00 a.m. - Noon, 1:00 p.m. - 5:00 p.m.

Guided tours only. The free tours begin at the top of each hour at the Interpretive Center and last approximately 45 minutes. The last tour begins at 4:00 p.m. Arrive before the hour at the Interpretive Center, sign up for your tour, and then you'll walk as a group over to the nearby museum. The maximum number of visitors on any given tour is eight, so be sure to arrive early if you are touring in the summer season.

Kam Wah Chung Interpretive Center
125 NW Canton St.
John Day, OR 97845
541-575-2800

Driving Directions: From SW Brent Drive, proceed west on Hwy 26 only a short distance to NW Canton Street. Turn right/north here and find the Kam Wah Chung Interpretive Center building on the right.

John Day Stop: Dine at the Snaffle Bit Dinner House

If you're hungry, then we recommend the Snaffle Bit Dinner House for great food served by nice folks. Enjoy ribs, burgers, seafood, chicken, pasta dishes, salads and, since you are in cattle country, tender and juicy steaks.

Snaffle Bit Dinner House
830 S Canyon Blvd.
John Day, OR 97845
541-575-2426

Hours:

- Monday through Friday: 12:00 p.m. to 9:00 p.m.
    - Winter Hours: 12:00 p.m. to 8:00 p.m.
- Closed Saturday and Sunday
- (Reservations recommended for dinner)

Driving Directions: From the Kam Wah Chung Interpretive Center, return to the Journey Through Time Scenic Byway / Hwy 26 and turn left / east. Travel east for 0.2 miles and turn right/south onto S Canyon Blvd./Hwy 395. Proceed south for 0.7 miles to the Snaffle Bit Dinner House on your left.

Next Stop: Oxbow Wagons & Coaches

Step through the door and back in time at Canyon City's Oxbow Wagons & Coaches. Building and restoring authentic carriages, buggies, stagecoaches, buckboards, chuckwagons and even sleighs, Oxbow Wagons & Coaches hand crafts and preserves the very vehicles used by pioneers throughout the west. You're welcome to stop by and peruse their shop, ask questions, look through the antiques, and see the large former dance hall filled with all kinds of horse-drawn vehicles from the past. Oh, and you'll see more wagon wheels here than you've ever seen in your lifetime!

Oxbow Wagons & Coaches is open daily, but it is best to call in advance to make sure they are not out delivering a vehicle.

> Oxbow Wagons & Coaches
> 303 S. Canyon City Blvd.
> Canyon City, OR 97820
> 541-575-2911

Driving Directions: From the Snaffle Bit Dinner House, drive south on Hwy 395 for 1.5 miles and find Oxbow Wagons & Coaches on your left.

Next Stop: Detour onto Burns - Izee Rd. / NF-47

Driving south out of John Day on the John Day - Burns Hwy / Hwy 395, you are now beginning to journey into remote southeastern Oregon with its stunning open vistas, fascinating geologic wonders, and rich historical heritage. While Hwy 395 will take you directly south to Burns, you'll instead detour along a less traveled road through the tall Ponderosa Pines of the Malheur National Forest before transitioning into open expanses with endless wheat fields, all under unending blue skies.

Driving Directions: From Oxbow Wagons & Coaches, drive south on Hwy 395 for 15.4 miles to "Izee - Paulina Ln." / Hwy 63. (May also be marked as "Izee Rd. to Bush Ranch Rd."/ Hwy 63 on your map, which leads to Izee, OR and Paulina, OR.) Turn right/west here and follow this for 23.5 miles to the intersection with Burns-Izee Road. (Note: You may be tempted to continue west to see Izee, but we found Izee Isn't. It's a beautiful drive, but Izee is only a couple of homes.) Follow Burns-Izee Road south for 46.7 miles until it connects with Hwy 20, south of Burns, OR. Turn left/north onto Hwy 20 and follow this 3 miles into Burns.

Next Stop: Burns, Oregon

The largest city in these parts, Burns is known as the gateway to the Steens Mountains. However, this isn't 100% accurate, as it is also the gateway to the Malheur National Wildlife Refuge, Diamond, Frenchglen, the Alvord Desert, the Pillars of Rome and, ultimately, the dramatic Leslie Gulch area, all areas you will be visiting during your road trip.

Burns is also a good place to stock up on any last minute supplies, including jugs of water, which are needed for camping at Leslie Gulch beginning tomorrow evening. Jordan Valley, OR has a *small* store at its gas station, as does Rome, OR, but in Burns you will find large grocery and hardware stores, as well as other suppliers.

Note: Fill your gas tank in Burns.

Next Stop: Malheur National Wildlife Refuge

A shaded oasis for migratory birds, as well as road travelers, the Malheur National Wildlife Refuge covers 293 square miles and is dedicated to protecting this important link in the long chain that is the Pacific Flyway, a migratory route used by over one billion birds annually and reaching from the Arctic tundra in Alaska's north all the way south to Patagonia in South America. *Photo courtesy of ShareOregon.com*

Stop at the headquarters, administered by the US Department of Fish & Wildlife, to enjoy its shaded grounds and to learn all about the vast refuge and its 320 different bird species, including Sandhill Cranes, Trumpeter Swans, Yellow-Headed Black Birds, Great Blue Herons, Great White Pelicans, Avocets, and many, many others. To see what will be "in town" during your visit, review the calendar for bird arrivals by visiting the Friends of Malheur National Wildlife Refuge web site at www.MalheurFriends.org/birding-and-wildlife/

Malheur National Wildlife Refuge
36391 Sodhouse Ln.
Princeton, OR 97721
541-493-2612

Driving Directions: Leaving Burns, you'll begin driving south on the High Desert Discovery Scenic Byway / Hwy 205. Proceed south out of Burns on Highway 205 and continue for approximately 25 miles to Narrows-Princeton Rd. Turn left/east here and follow this for 6 miles as it becomes Sodhouse Ln. before eventually reaching the Malheur National Wildlife Refuge.

TONIGHT'S LODGING-
HISTORIC HOTEL DIAMOND
DIAMOND, OR

Tonight's stay is at the iconic Hotel Diamond, 52 miles south of Burns. Built in 1898, it sits beneath tall Poplar trees standing amidst amber wheat fields punctuated by small rocky bluffs, and because Diamond has a population of only five people, one might consider Hotel Diamond to be the center of town...where you alone make up 15% of the population. Beautiful, remote and peaceful...Oregon.

Built for utility over 120 years ago, though now renovated, guests can choose from five small rooms upstairs, all sharing a common bathroom, as well as three "newer" rooms downstairs, all of which are larger and come with a private bath.

In addition to the rooms, guests may enjoy dinner at the hotel for a reasonable price. Meals are served family style in the dining room around one or more tables, and you will be joined

by fellow travelers, which can make for excellent conversation as you share your stories from the road. Note that dinner is served at 6:30 p.m., and reservations need to be made at least one day in advance. A ranch-style breakfast of eggs, sausage, ham, biscuits, fruit and more is included with the cost of your room, and it is served family style, as well. Accommodations are made as much as possible for gluten-free and lactose intolerant guests, though please let your hosts know of your needs when making your reservations.

Note: You'll often see large Great Horned Owls sitting in the rafters of the old stone building outside the Hotel Diamond, as well as in the nearby Poplar trees. Approach the building quietly before slowly peeking into the windows.

Historic Hotel Diamond
49130 Main St.
Diamond, OR 97722
541-493-1898

www.HistoricHotelDiamond.com

Driving Directions: From the Malheur Wildlife Refuge - Return west to the junction with the High Desert Discovery Scenic Byway / Hwy 205. From here, drive south 16.8 miles and turn left/west onto Diamond Ln. Follow this 12.3 miles to Diamond.

Day Five

Diamond to Leslie Gulch

Day 5
Diamond Loop Tour Route – to Leslie Gulch

Day 5 – Date: / /

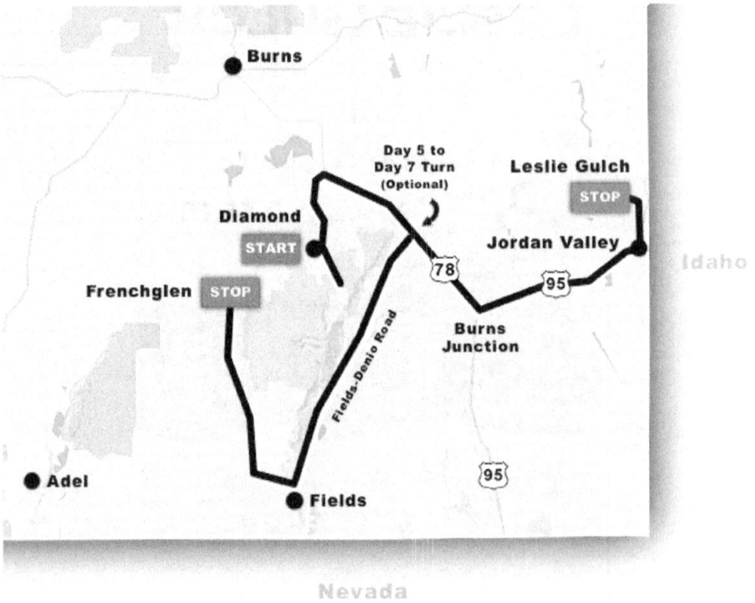

Summary: Where You're Going Today

- Diamond, OR
- Kiger Mustang Herd Management Area
- Pete French Round Barn
- Rome
- Jordan Valley
- Leslie Gulch

Today, you'll leave Diamond on the Diamond Loop Tour Route before heading southeast on Hwy 78, and then east on Hwy 95, to the welcoming town of Jordan Valley. After a brief refueling, you'll then drive north on Hwy 95 to beautiful Leslie Gulch.

Tonight's Lodging:

There are no reservations needed today if you are camping at Leslie Gulch this evening and the next. However, if you are planning to explore Leslie Gulch, but instead wish to stay overnight in the town of Jordan Valley, OR during the nights of Day 5 and Day 6, instead of camping *in* Leslie Gulch, then you will need to make lodging reservations for those two nights. Note that, as of the time of this publication, lodging options in the town of Jordan Valley are *very* limited and possibly non-existent, as businesses open and close. See page 109 for additional details.

Option: If you do not wish to camp at or explore Leslie Gulch at all, but instead travel only as far east as Fields-Denio Road / East Steens Tour Route before turning south to Fields, OR, then you will be jumping from Day 5 to the middle of Day 7 when you make that turn, which works just fine. In doing so, you will cut out the leg to Jordan Valley and Leslie Gulch, and be shortening your trip by two days. As a result, you will be staying the next two evenings not at Leslie Gulch, but instead at the Frenchglen Hotel, where reservations for your stay *and 6:30 p.m. dinner are required.* See the map on page 104 and information on pages 116, 129 and 130 for additional details.

Today's Mileage: 188 Miles

Start

BTW, have you made your reservations for the 6:30 pm dinner(s) at the Frenchglen Hotel on Days 7 & 8 yet? 541-493-2825

Today involves scenery, exploring, adventure, and a bit of driving. Begin the day with an adventurous trek out to the very remote Kiger Mustang Herd Management Area, and then return to civilization with a stop at the Pete French Round Barn before setting out on a scenic two hour drive east to Jordan Valley, where you'll turn north toward Leslie Gulch. Here, you'll settle in for two nights of camping in an amazing Oregon landscape.

First Stop: Kiger Mustang Herd Management Area

This next stop is for only the adventurous who *respect* the journey and appreciate the destination.

Traveling east on Happy Valley Road for approximately 3.6 miles from Diamond, you'll come to a road that veers to the right, and just off the main road is a large Bureau of Land Management sign which reads *Kiger Mustang Herd Management Area - 11 Miles.* (photo) Shortly thereafter is another sign, which reads *Rough Road - Passenger Cars Not Recommended.* What follows is an adventure well off the grid and deep into the remote.

- Warning: You could get stuck or stranded
- Warning: You may damage the underside of your car
- Warning: You are on your own
- Warning: You will have no cell signal
- Warning: There may be nobody else around for miles
- Note: With a bit of caution, a *proper* well-maintained car, food and water, and common sense, you may be just fine.

Following this road takes you to the Kiger Mustang Herd Management area where you may...or may not...see the beautiful and rare wild Kiger Mustangs. Look for them as you travel for 11 miles along this rough road to a viewpoint, which is guaranteed to offer a stunning vista of Southeast Oregon. Note: Do not drive the last 50 yards, but instead walk up to the viewpoint.

Kristy and I drove this road in our Audi allroad, and we were just fine, save for that one rock that I thought I could drive over. It turned out I couldn't, and it bent an exhaust support under my car, requiring a trip to the repair shop. All I had to do was stop the car, get out, and toss the rock aside, but noooo, I decided to take my chances to save time. Stupid rock.

Important! DO NOT drive this road if it is muddy or the skies are threatening to rain, as water makes Southeast Oregon's roads very slippery, *and there is a likelihood you will get stuck.*

Directions: Leave the Diamond Hotel and travel east on Happy Valley Road. In approximately ¼ mile, Happy Valley Road splits. Take the road to the left/north, and continue for approximately 3.6 miles as it winds east until you come to a road that veers off to the right, forming a large "Y". Look for the sign on the previous page to confirm you have the right road, and then take this road to the Kiger Mustang Herd Management Area, which terminates at an overlook in 11 miles.

Next Stop: Pete French Round Barn

An Oregon icon unique in both its appearance and location, the Pete French Round Barn is a nearly 150 year-old barn that is perfectly round. Here, beginning in the late 1880s, Peter French and others would train and break between 300 to 1,000 horses every year, many during the cold Southeast Oregon winters while taking advantage of the barn's enclosed circular shape.

Nearby, visitors will find an interpretive center and very nice gift shop showcasing many of the items used by pioneers of the area, as well as residents in the early to mid-20th century. Water, snacks and clean restrooms are also available here.

Driving Directions: Return to the junction with Happy Valley Rd. and turn right/east. Follow Happy Valley Rd. for approximately 9 miles until it merges with Diamond Craters Rd. north. Then proceed only a short distance to the large sign and turnoff for the Pete French Round Barn and visitor center.

Next Stop: Jordan Valley, OR

Your next stop is at Jordan Valley, which is 117 miles (2 Hours) to the southeast from the Pete French Round Barn. You'll stop here to get gas, water and perhaps lunch or dinner before driving north for 50 miles to camp at Leslie Gulch. Note that there is no potable water in Leslie Gulch.

Note: It is important that you get gas in Jordan Valley before leaving for Leslie Gulch, as gas will not be available until you return this way. The gas station is open 24 hours a day, 365 days a year. (541-586-2244) Note, as well, that restaurant choices are limited in Jordan Valley. Be sure to check out Skinner's Rockhouse Coffee, and Boise, ID is 1.5 hours away via Hwy 95.

Driving Directions: Return from the Pete French Round Barn to Diamond Craters Road. Turn right/north onto the Diamond Loop Tour Route / Diamond Craters Road and proceed 10.5 miles to Narrows-Princeton Rd. / Sodhouse Ln. Turn right/east and drive for 3 miles to Hwy 78. Turn right/southeast onto Hwy 78 and proceed 51.5 miles to Burns Junction. Merge left/east onto Hwy 95 at Burns Junction and continue 45 miles to Jordan Valley, OR. Note: There is gas and food available in Rome, 12.7 miles past Burns Junction, ½ hour west of Jordan Valley. (Rome Station - Page 128)

Jordan Valley Stop: Flat Iron Steakhouse & Inn

Note: It used to be that the Flat Iron Steakhouse & Inn on Wroten Street offered a nice alternative to camping in Leslie Gulch. You'd simply stay at the inn on the nights of Day 5 and Day 6, and then drive north during the day to explore Leslie Gulch. Unfortunately, the inn closed due to the pandemic, and it was still closed at the time of this publication. Because the building is still there, and it may reopen under new ownership sometime in the future, we've decided to leave information about the inn in this guidebook. When planning your trip, check online to see if it has perhaps reopened, provided you do not wish to camp in Leslie Gulch.

Prior to closing, the inn on Wroten Street offered burgers, steaks, seafood, salads, milkshakes, desserts and more, as well as gluten free options. In addition, being an inn, they offered four clean rooms for rent. Two had queen-sized beds, and two had double-sized, and they all shared a bathroom with a shower down the hall. Breakfasts were also available.

306 Wroten St.
Jordan Valley, OR 97910
541-586-2800

Jordan Valley Stop: Traditional Basque Pelota Fronton Handball Court

Located near the juncture of Hwy 95 and Bassett Street is a structure more than 100 years old that resembles the walls of a former two story building. However, it is actually a tribute to the large population of Basque immigrants who used to reside in the Jordan Valley area. Restored in 1997 and listed on the National Register of Historic Places, the walls you see here make up a Pelota Fronton court, used by the Basque immigrants to play Pelota, a traditional sport similar to today's squash or racquetball. Learn more about the court at the interpretive sign posted nearby.

Jordan Valley Stop: Interesting Architecture

To the east of the gas station in Jordan Valley is an interesting example of mid-20th century architecture, the Sahara Motel. Unfortunately, it closed quite some time ago.

Tonight's Lodging - Camping At Leslie Gulch

This amazing segment of your road trip is comprised of a unique Oregon adventure set in one of the most remote and stunning parts of the state. For the next two nights you'll be camping in Leslie Gulch.

Located amongst dramatic rock features, the Slocum Creek Campground of Leslie Gulch sits at the end of a 15 mile dirt road lined by towering rock cliffs, mysterious honeycombed walls, and awe-inspiring rock features formed from colorful volcanic ash carved by the powerful and relentless forces of nature. Nearby, the wide Owyhee River flows slowly, giving life to an abundance of flora and fauna, including over 200 Bighorn Sheep, Mule Deer, Bobcats, Coyotes, Mountain Elk, Great Horned Owls, California Quail, and bats, as well as seasonal wildflowers, including the colorful Arrowleaf Balsamroot, Indian Paintbrush and Lupine.

During your visit, you can tour the Leslie Gulch area, as well as explore a number of hikes to dramatic geologic features and impressive vistas, all while keeping an eye out for wildlife. In addition, when the sun goes down, the stars come out, filling the night sky with an abundance of stars about 45 minutes after sunset. It is a somewhat rare sight to see, as there is no light pollution in this remote area to obscure your view of the heavens.

Campground Specs:

- There are 10 Camp sites - Those closest to the river receive the first morning light.
- Each site contains a picnic table, a sun shelter and a fire pit.
- No reservations or fees are required - The sites are first come, first served.
- No water or electricity is available - Be sure to bring your own water and a light source. Don't forget fresh batteries.
- Nice pit toilets are available.
- No Wi-Fi or cell signals are available.
- The campground is open from March through November.

Campground Notes:

- There is little to no privacy or seclusion at this campsite, though that is part of the experience. It's a great way to meet fellow travelers.

- Spots are usually available, even during busy holiday weekends, including Labor Day, in which perhaps only half the sites are occupied. However, spots can become few during the spring fishing season.

- Campfires are allowed, but call the local BLM office (541-473-3144) if you are camping late in the dry season to see if any restrictions are currently in effect. This may save you from hauling wood during your trip, which you cannot burn. There is no downed wood available in Leslie Gulch.

- Be mindful of ticks, rattlesnakes and goat heads (weeds), especially when off road or off trail.

    - Goat heads are abundant within each campsite. Smaller than your fingernail, each of these rock hard seed heads brandish multiple sharp points that can *easily* puncture most materials, including your air mattress. Be sure to bring one or more extra tarps as well as extra blankets to place under your tent and air mattress so as to create a layer thick enough that the goat heads cannot reach your mattress. Of course, do your best to clear your tent site of these small irritants before you put down your tent, and if you have some time, spend a moment digging up any of these invasive plants and put them in your fire pit, whether you're having a fire or not.

A Goat Head

    - It would be wise to bring an air mattress patching kit, just in case.

- Important! Goat head seeds are not kind to dog paws or bike tires. Be mindful of this when traveling off road, and be sure to bring along a bike tube repair kit when mountain biking.

- Fishing is very popular in this area, given the Owyhee River is so close. Note, however, that all species of fish within the river have high levels of mercury due to volcanic deposits.

- Summer months can be exceptionally warm, with the average temperature in August being 90 degrees. Be sure to bring plenty of water, a sun hat, sunscreen, and sunglasses for your trip.

We have listed some things to simply be mindful of when camping here, *but none of these should stop you from experiencing this unique Oregon adventure.*

Slocum Creek Campground
Leslie Gulch Road
Jordan Valley, OR 97910

Bureau of Land Management, Vale, OR: 541-473-3144

Driving Directions to Slocum Creek Campground:

(You're in for some fantastic scenery!) From Jordan Valley - Proceed north out of Jordan Valley on Hwy 95 for approximately 18 miles to Succor Creek Road. Turn left/west onto Succor Creek Road and drive northwest for 10 miles before reaching Leslie Gulch Road. Turn left/west onto Leslie Gulch Road and follow this down into Leslie Gulch for 14 miles on a well maintained gravel road to the Slocum Creek Campground.

Camping Options

Camping Option #1 - Succor Creek Campground:

Note: Camping at the Slocum Creek Campground takes a bit of a commitment on your part, as it may be full when you arrive. That said, Kristy and I have camped here during Labor Day Weekend, and the campground was only half full. If it is full, you may find campsites available at Succor Creek Campground and State Park, approximately 28 miles to the northwest.

Succor Creek Campground

- 18 Primitive campsites - 12 tent-only sites are on the east side of the creek, accessible by a footbridge.
- Picnic tables and a pit toilet are available on the west side of the creek.
- No electricity or water is available, though you can treat water from the creek.

Driving Directions:

Drive back east on Leslie Gulch Road until it intersects in a "T" with Succor Creek Road. Turn left/north and follow this 10 miles to the Succor Creek State Natural Area. Note that Succor Creek Road becomes narrow after leaving Leslie Gulch Road. As a result, trailers and RVs are not recommended. It is possible to continue back out to Highway 95 and follow this north to Homedale, Idaho, taking Highway 201 west out of Homedale for approximately 6.5 miles until it connects with Succor Creek Road heading south, which will lead you to Succor Creek State Natural Area. In other words, you will be approaching Succor Creek Campground from the north, instead of from the south.

Camping Option #2:

Consider returning to Jordan Valley and getting a room at the local inn, *if it is open and operating.* If it is late in the day, you'll want to call them as soon as you have a cell signal.

Camping Option #3:

If you prefer not to camp nor travel out to Jordan Valley and Leslie Gulch, you may depart from the Pete French Round Barn on Day 5 and jump directly to mid-day on Day 7, where you'll turn right/south off of Highway 78 and travel along Fields-Denio Road toward Fields, OR before turning north to Frenchglen. See the map on page 104, as well as pages 129 and 130 for details. Note that this will shorten your road trip by two days.

Driving Directions for skipping Jordan Valley and skipping camping at Leslie Gulch:

Departing from the Pete French Round Barn on page 107...

Return from the Pete French Round Barn to Diamond Craters Road. Turn right/north onto the Diamond Loop Tour Route / Diamond Craters Road and proceed 10.5 miles to Narrows-Princeton Rd. / Sodhouse Ln. Turn right/east and drive for 3 miles to Hwy 78. Turn right/southeast onto Hwy 78 and proceed approximately 25 miles to Fields-Denio Road. Turn right/south onto Fields-Denio Road towards Fields, OR. At this turn, you will be turning from Day 5 to the middle of Day 7.

NOTES

Day Six

Explore Leslie Gulch

DAY 6
EXPLORE LESLIE GULCH

Day 6 – Date: / /

Today involves very little driving. Instead, you'll stay closer to home as you explore the geologic wonders of Leslie Gulch.

Today's Activities: Leslie Gulch Hikes

Note: Leslie Gulch is a high desert area. As such, temperatures can become extreme during the hot summer months, so it is important to wear a hat, sunscreen and sunglasses, as well as stay hydrated during your hikes. Be mindful of rattlesnakes and ticks for yourself, as well as your pet.

Juniper Gulch Hike

This popular 0.8 mile hike captures the geologic essence of Leslie Gulch. Make your way up an easy trail before gaining an amphitheater surrounded by an abundance of desert colors, intriguing shapes and evidence of powerful geologic forces at work.

The trail splits at about the 1/2 mile mark. Follow the trail right up to an amphitheater and then continue left for another 3/4 mile as the trail steepens and winds its way up to a ridgeline, which rewards hikers with views of the Owyhee Canyonlands and Lake Owyhee.

Easy to moderate - 400' of elevation gain.

Trailhead Directions: Located approximately 3.3 miles east of Slocum Creek Campground. The trailhead is well signed on the north side of the main road through Leslie Gulch and has space for several cars. A restroom is available here.

Timber Gulch Hike

This is an excellent moderate hike, and if your timing is right, you'll enjoy a unique reward that is sure to be a highlight of your trip.

The Timber Gulch hike is along more of a route than a trail, with sizeable step ups and brief climbs along the way, but this only makes it more adventurous and the payoff is worth it, especially in the early to mid-morning or late afternoon when the direct and ambient lighting dramatically plays off the stone walls.

Hike the .8 mile trail to the amphitheater sometime in the early to mid-morning and find a boulder to sit upon while you take in the amazing geology all around you. About this time of day, you may be rewarded with a highlight of your trip as hundreds, if not thousands, of small birds (Swifts?) descend out of the large vertical crack found in the rock face to the north. (Photo) Listen for small flocks of birds calling as they fly quickly out of the amphitheater and then simply track them back to where they come from and you'll find the crack. Be in this same spot late in the evening and you'll see them all fly back into the crack before settling in for the night.

1.2 Miles round trip - 350' of elevation gain - Moderate

Trailhead Directions: Located a little over 2 miles east of Slocum Creek Campground. The trailhead for the Timber Gulch trail head is not marked. Instead, look for a small pullout on the north side of the road, large enough for only two cars. The trail starts directly from the pullout.

Dago Gulch Hike

An easy 1.6 mile round trip hike takes you up an open road grade, where you can explore nearby steep canyons to see amazing geologic features.

190' elevation gain - Easy

Trailhead Directions: Located 4.3 miles east of Slocum Creek Campground. Park at the large open trailhead, just south of the main road through Leslie Gulch.

Next Stop: Return to Camp

Camp for your second night at Leslie Gulch.

NOTES

Day Seven

Leslie Gulch to Frenchglen

DAY 7
LESLIE GULCH TO FRENCHGLEN

Day 7 – Date: / /

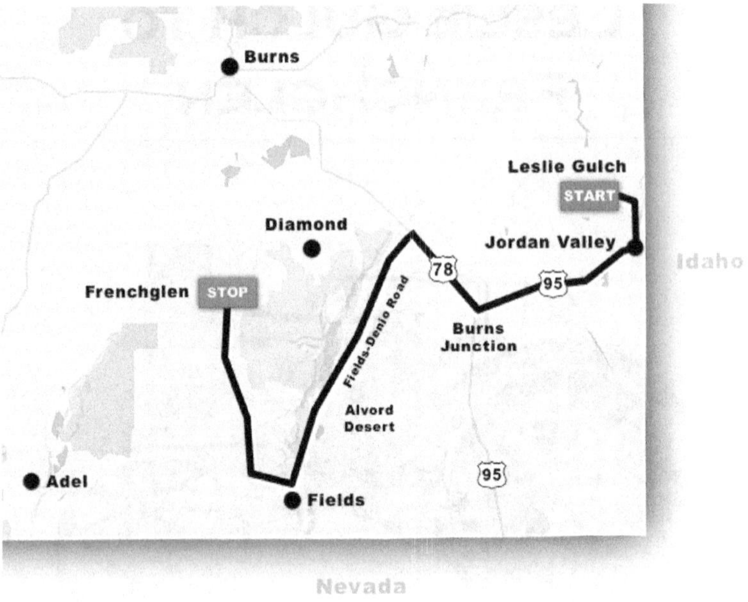

Summary: Where You're Going Today

- Leslie Gulch
- Jordan Valley, OR
- Owyhee Overlook
- Pillars of Rome
- East Steens
- Alvord Desert
- Fields, OR
- Frenchglen, OR

With today's journey, you'll leave the narrow canyons of Leslie Gulch and make your way back west, turning south toward Steens Mountain, a massive escarpment rising over 5,000 feet above the Alvord Desert to a height of nearly 10,000 feet.

Tonight's Lodging:

- The Frenchglen Hotel

Today's Mileage: 231 Miles

Reservations Needed for This Segment:

- The Frenchglen Hotel - 2 Nights - 541-493-2825
- Dinner at the Frenchglen Hotel - Dinner is optional, but if you chose to eat at the hotel, you must make reservations *at least one day in advance.* Dinner is promptly served at 6:30 p.m. Note that space in the dining room can become limited at times, and preference is given to hotel guests when this occurs. Dining options are very limited in Frenchglen.

Start

Today's schedule will hinge upon two things; 6:30 p.m. dinner reservations at the Frenchglen Hotel, if you made them, *or* the fact that you'll need to reach Fields Station by 3:30 p.m. if you didn't make reservations and still want to eat. Fields Station, in Fields, OR, takes its last dinner order at 3:30 p.m. Milkshakes by 5:00 p.m. Oh, and you can't get gas there after 6:00 p.m. All that said, you should have time in your schedule today to either get up and rolling at a leisurely pace or begin your day with a short hike in Leslie Gulch before heading out.

First Stop: Return to Jordan Valley

Fill your gas tank in Jordan Valley.

Next Stop: Owyhee Canyon Overlook

Your remote Southeast Oregon experience continues as you explore wide open scenery south of Hwy 95 and discover the impressive Owyhee Canyon, a deep cliff-lined gorge home to the Owyhee River far below. Note: The drive out to the overlook is very scenic, as well.

Driving Directions: From Leslie Gulch, return to Jordan Valley. Drive west on Hwy 95 from Jordan Valley for approximately 15 miles and look for a small sign for 3 Forks Road. Turn left/south from Hwy 95 onto the 3 Forks Road and follow this dirt and gravel road for 16.5 scenic miles to a large sign announcing the overlook. Note: The dirt and gravel road is well maintained, though you do not want to travel it if it is wet or rain is threatening, as it is likely you will become stuck.

Next Stop: Rome Station

A welcome shady oasis, Rome Station offers travelers a menu of burgers, shakes, fries, ice cream, and snacks, as well as services for the road, including ice, gas, motor oil and towing. An RV park and cabins are also available.

Rome Station
3605 US-95
Jordan Valley, OR 97910
541-586-2295

Driving Directions: Return to the intersection with Hwy 95 and turn left/west toward Rome. Follow Hwy 95 for approximately 17 miles to Rome Station.

Next Stop: Pillars of Rome

Your next stop takes you to Rome, Italy via an Oregon geologic wonder. Journey a couple miles north of Hwy 95 and there you'll find the "Pillars of Rome", a unique formation of brittle fossil-bearing clay towers reaching 100' high, which bear a resemblance to the ancient ruined temples of Rome, Italy.

Driving Directions: From Rome Station, drive back east on Hwy 95 a little over one hundred feet to Rome Road. Turn left/northwest onto Rome Road and follow this 1.8 miles to Old Ion Hwy. Turn right onto Old Ion Hwy and in 0.3 miles turn left/west onto Kiger Road. Follow Kiger Road anywhere from 1 to 1.5 miles to the Pillars of Rome. Note that there does not appear to be a trailhead for access to the pillars, and we had to enjoy them from a distance behind a barbed wire fence.

Next Stop: Fields-Denio Road/East Steens Tour Route

Turning south off Hwy 78, you'll journey onto Fields-Denio Road, which is also part of the scenic East Steens Road Tour Route. To the west, you'll see the magnificent Steens Mountain escarpment stretching for 30 miles and rising 5,000' above you to become the highest point in Southeast Oregon at nearly 10,000'. As you traverse its impressive base, keep in mind you'll be standing near its summit tomorrow!

Driving Directions: From the Pillars of Rome - Return to Hwy 95 and proceed west. Continue to Burns Junction, where you will take Hwy 78 northwest. Proceed 27 miles from Burns Junction and then turn left/south onto Fields - Denio Road / East Steens Road at the sign that reads "Andrews 51 - Fields 65". Follow this to Fields, OR. Note, a good portion of this road is well-maintained gravel.

If You Are Skipping Camping At Leslie Gulch

If you are choosing to jump from Day 5 to this point in Day 7, thus skipping two days of camping and exploring Leslie Gulch, then you will want to turn south onto Fields - Denio Road / East Steens Road here (above) and resume your trip with the next stop. (Below)

Next Stop: Alvord Desert

After traveling south on Fields-Denio Road for approximately 30 miles, you'll begin to see Oregon's Alvord Desert to the east. Actually a large lake bed, it lies in the "rain shadow" of the Cascades and Steens Mountain ranges, receiving only 7" of rain annually, which is only 1/10th that received by Mt. Hood! Springtime delivers the most rainfall, while summer brings some of the hottest temperatures in the state. Scattered around its edges are a small handful of hot springs and geothermal features. There are a number of access points, some of which are free, but travelers may also pay a fee to access the desert at the Alvord Hot Springs, which is your next stop. *(Photo © Jim Moore)*

Next Stop: Alvord Hot Springs

Situated in the scenic wide open spaces between the base of Steens Mountain and the Alvord Desert is the Alvord Hot Springs, made up of two 10' x 12' concrete lined pools in a rustic setting with wooden decking and a bench. Water emerges from a nearby spring at a scalding hot 170 degrees, but is cooled by a set of pipes to keep the pools near 112 degrees Fahrenheit. Formerly free to the public, the hot springs are now privately owned, maintained, and monitored so as to prevent vandalism. In addition, services, such as camping, showers, RV parking and a small store, are now available. If you wish to use the hot springs, check in at the store upon your arrival.

Alvord Hot Springs
36095 E Steens Rd.
New Princeton, OR 97721 (541-589-2282)

Note: The hot springs are approximately 69 miles south of New Princeton, OR.

Note: After parking, do not get out and begin walking across the "field" to the hot springs, but instead always stay on the main path. There is the possibility that you could break through the field crust and scald your feet on hot water beneath the surface. Pets should always be on a leash, as well.

Driving Directions: Look for the large sign for the Alvord Hot Springs on your left approximately 41.5 miles after you turned south onto Fields - Denio Road / East Steens Road.

Next Stop: Fields, Oregon

First operating as a stagecoach supply station beginning in 1881, today Fields Station in Fields, Oregon serves as a diner, small market, hardware store, motel, gas station and post office, providing much needed supplies and service to sightseers, hunters, fishermen, pilots and more who drive, ride and fly to this remote southeast corner of our state. In addition to providing 87 octane gas, diesel, propane, ice, and more, Fields Station also serves excellent breakfasts, lunches and dinners, including burgers, fries and "world famous" milkshakes. Note, however, that orders must be in by 3:30 p.m., as dinner stops being served at 4:00 p.m.

- Dinner: Order by 3:30 p.m. - Milkshakes by 5:00 p.m.
- Gas: Fill up by 6:00 p.m. (5:00 p.m. on Sundays)

Top off your gas here - 87 Octane and Diesel. Frenchglen is 52 miles to the north.

The Fields Station
22276 Fields Drive
Fields, OR 97710 (541-495-2275)

Lodging is also available at Fields Station. Two pet-friendly rooms are available, as well as a third larger room, and they are clean and comfortable with private baths and air-conditioning.

Driving Directions: From the Alvord Desert Hot Springs, drive south on East Steens Road for 23 miles to Fields, OR.

Tonight's Lodging - The Frenchglen Hotel Frenchglen, OR

Situated where the Malheur Wildlife Refuge meets Steens Mountain, the quaint and historic 1923 Frenchglen Hotel is actually a state park that welcomes visitors with a taste of the old west combined with Southeast Oregon hospitality.

Visitors may choose from five small quaint rooms in the hotel itself, all featuring old west furnishings done in a clean and tasteful style, and all without TVs...just the way you want it. Shared baths are just down the hallway. Out back, five additional rooms accommodate guests at Drovers' Inn, which was built to accommodate guest overflow from the Frenchglen Hotel. This is a modern facility with larger rooms, queen-sized beds, air-conditioning and private baths. Note that the one room upstairs is a bit larger than the others downstairs.

For breakfast and dinner, you'll eat with fellow travelers around family-style tables in the main lobby area, which is a fun way to share stories of life on the road, as well as pick up the latest tips about tomorrow's adventure...driving the Steens Mountain Loop road.

- Breakfast: 7:30 a.m. to 9:30 a.m. - Priced $6.50 to $13.50
- Lunch: 11:30 a.m. to 2:30 p.m. - Priced $10.00 - $15.00
- Family Style Dinner: $25.00 to $30.00 - *Reservations are required and must be made at least one day in advance. Dinner is served promptly at 6:30 p.m.*

Sack lunches to go are also available, and can be perfect for your trip to Steens Mountain. Please let the hotel know the evening before if you'd like a sack lunch the next day.

Note: You are making reservations for **two nights**. The Frenchglen Hotel is open seasonally, from March 15th to November 1st, while the Drovers' inn is open all year. Cancellations require at least 72 hours advance notice.

Frenchglen Hotel State Heritage Site
39184 Hwy 205
Frenchglen, OR 97736

541-493-2825
FGHotel@Yahoo.com

Driving Directions: From Fields, OR - Drive north on East Steens Road for 1.4 miles to the exit for Hwy 205. Turn left/northwest onto Hwy 205 and follow this 51 miles as it takes you directly to Frenchglen, OR and the Frenchglen Hotel.

Lodging Options

Steens Mountain Wilderness Resort

While we have not visited here, nearby is the Steens Mountain Wilderness Resort, which offers nine rental units with kitchens, private baths and heating and cooling units. Some offer modest accommodations requiring you to bring your own bedding and towels, while others are more full-service, complete with TVs and a washer and dryer set.

Directions: Located on the same road as the Page Springs Campground below.

Steens Mountain Wilderness Resort
35678 Resort Lane
Frenchglen, OR 97736 (541-493-2415)
www.SteensMountainResort.com

Steens View Cabin

Located close to the Frenchglen Hotel, the beautiful (and newer) Steens View Cabin offers guests 3 bedrooms, 2 bathrooms, a full kitchen, washer & dryer, and more.

Steens View Cabin
42704 Artemisia Road
Frenchglen, OR 97736
www.SteensViewCabin.com

Page Springs Campground

Camping is also available at the nearby Page Springs Campground, a nice facility with 36 camping spaces on soft green grass shaded by Cottonwood and fir trees. Available year-round.

Directions: Travel east of Frenchglen for 3.6 miles on the Steens Mountain Loop Road, which can be accessed immediately southeast of Frenchglen.

Day Eight

Steens Mountain Tour Loop

Day 8
Steens Mountain Tour Loop

Day 8 – Date: / /

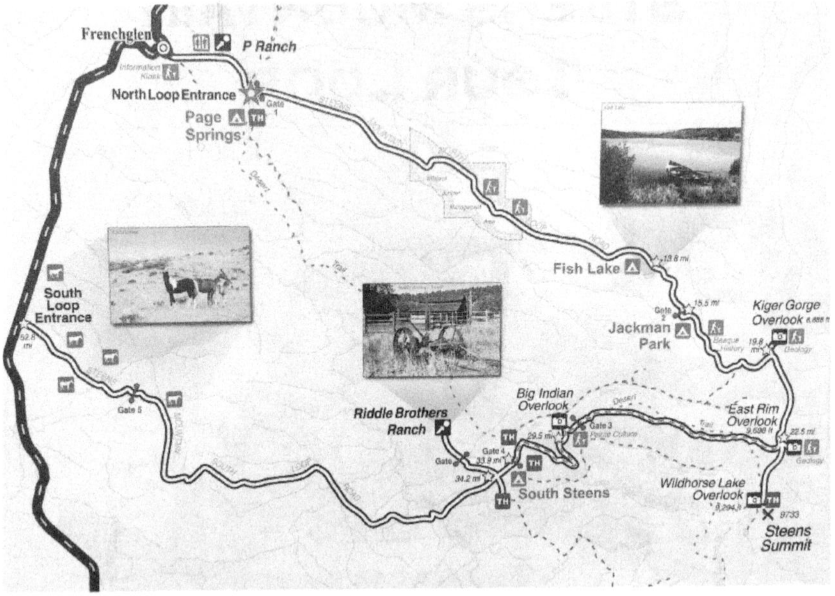

Summary: Where You're Going Today

Today, you'll drive the dramatic Steens Mountain Tour Loop, the highest road in all of Oregon. This well maintained road leaves Frenchglen and winds its way up and up past numerous scenic stopping points, finally taking you to the 9,734' summit and beyond before winding its way back to Frenchglen, where you'll stay a second night at the Frenchglen Hotel. *If you're having dinner this evening at 6:30 p.m., be sure to let your hosts know.*

Note: As a point of reference, we started traveling today at 10:00 a.m. and finished back at Frenchglen by 5:00 p.m.

Note: You'll want to bring a warm jacket and clothing, even during the summer months, as you will be driving to nearly 10,000' in elevation, where it will be much cooler and likely windy. In addition, bring camp chairs for having lunch when you reach Big Indian Gorge.

The *entire* Steens Mountain Tour Loop can remain closed well into late spring or early summer due to snow, often opening on July 4th weekend. Ask about the current road conditions when making your hotel reservation. The road will usually close again sometime in November or December. For the latest "official" road conditions, call the Burns, OR Bureau of Land Management office at 541-573-4400.

Tonight's Lodging:

- You will stay a second night at the Frenchglen Hotel.

Reservations Needed for This Segment:

- No reservations are needed for today. However, if you wish to bring a sack lunch made by the Frenchglen Hotel during your drive, you'll need to notify them the evening before. *In addition, if you're planning on having dinner at the hotel this evening at 6:30 p.m., be sure to let your hosts know this when you make your room reservations.*

Today's Mileage: 70 Miles Round-trip

Note: Fill your tank at the nearby Frenchglen Mercantile, just north of the hotel. If the gas trickles out slowly when you first squeeze the handle, then flip the lever on the side of the pump up and down twice. There is no gas available along today's route. By the way, this gas pump should look pretty familiar to you by now, as it is the gas pump icon found throughout this book!

Frenchglen Mercantile
39212 Highway 205
Frenchglen, OR 97736
541-493-2564

- Hours: 9:00 a.m. to 6:00 p.m - Monday - Sunday.
- Open April/May to November.

First Stop: Kiger Gorge Overlook

Park your car and walk a short distance to see the striking Kiger Gorge, a massive U-shaped valley over 6,500' wide and more than 2,600' deep. Its rugged cliff sides are home to many different species of birds, including the Golden Eagle. Keep an eye out for this majestic bird as it soars *below* you.

Note: Be mindful of children and pets near the overlook cliffs. The Kiger Gorge is one of four gorges on Steens Mountain, including Kiger Gorge, Wildhorse, Big Indian and Little Blitzen.

Driving Directions: From the Frenchglen Hotel, drive south only a short distance and veer left onto the Steens Mountain Loop Tour road. Follow the signs for the Steens Mountain Loop Tour and begin ascending Steens Mountain, continuing 22.5 miles to the turnoff for the Kiger Gorge Overlook. Turn left/north toward the overlook and park in the parking area ¼ mile off the main road.

Next Stop: East Rim Viewpoint

Step out to the edge of the East Rim Viewpoint and look down over 5,000' to the Alvord Desert and all of far southeastern Oregon, Idaho and Nevada as it unfolds below you. This is another viewpoint which begs for binoculars.

Driving Directions: Drive back to the main loop road from the Kiger Gorge Overlook and continue east/southeast, ascending for another 2.7 miles. Turn left at the sign for the East Rim Viewpoint and proceed for 0.3 miles to parking area.

Next Stop: Steens Summit Area

Driving Directions: Continue south on the main loop road from the East Rim Viewpoint to the summit area and park in the gravel parking area where the road terminates, approximately ½ mile short of the summit.

Steens Summit Trail:

From the summit area parking lot follow the rocky road at the southern end of the lot up and to the left until you reach the summit area in less than ½ mile. Being just shy of 10,000' at this point, there is a good chance it will be windy here, so dress accordingly.

Note: You will likely have an excellent cell signal here, both in the parking lot and the summit area.

Wildhorse Lake Trail:

Leaving from the parking area and descending 1,200' to the southwest is the trail to Wildhorse Lake. Tucked into the picturesque cirque of Wildhorse Canyon, the lake showcases the impressive geology of the area and is an outstanding destination in the spring and summer when wildflowers are present.

Note: You'll be hiking at an elevation of above 8,500' for the entire distance to the lake and back. As such, unless you're in excellent physical condition, the hiking will likely be much more difficult than that you'd experience at a lower elevation. Keep in mind that the most difficult section of the hike will be the uphill portion of your return.

Photo © William L. Sullivan, www.OregonHiking.com

Next Stop: Big Indian Gorge

As you drive the descent from the Steens Mountain summit area, you'll pass along the impressive Big Indian Gorge. Making your way to the far end of the gorge, you'll see a turnout on your left where you can park near some trees. Stop here, set up a couple of camp chairs and enjoy the view overlooking the gorge while having a snack or perhaps your lunch.

Driving Directions: Leave the parking area for the Steens Summit Area and drive back north for 2 miles to Steens Mountain Road. Turn left/west here and begin your descent of Steens Mountain, along Big Indian Gorge and toward Hwy 205. You'll find the turnout mentioned above at approximately 9 miles from where you parked at the summit area.

Next Stop: Little Blitzen Gorge Trail

This hike is an opportunity to get out and immerse yourself in the flora, fauna and terrain of lower Steens Mountain.

Park at the trailhead parking lot on your left and you'll find the trailhead directly across the road. Follow the trail as it winds north through Juniper trees before descending to Little Blitzen River at about the one mile point. Step on stones to cross here and then continue to the right as the trail begins to pass through tall grasses and brush before meandering through Cottonwoods on its way along the river up and into the entrance of Little Blitzen Gorge, soon reaching 4-Mile Camp with its shaded streamside meadow.

Note: Keep in mind your schedule if you have reservations for the 6:30 p.m. dinner at the Frenchglen Hotel. The trailhead for this hike is approximately 30 miles from the hotel, two thirds of which are on slower roads.

Driving Directions: You'll find the large parking area for the Little Blitzen Gorge Trail at 4 miles beyond your last stop and 13 miles from the summit area.

Next Stop: The Frenchglen Hotel

Stay your second night at the Frenchglen Hotel.

Driving Directions: Continue 19.5 miles from the Little Blitzen Trailhead (32.5 miles from the Steens Mountain Summit Area) to Hwy 205. Turn right/north onto Highway 205 and follow this 10 miles directly into Frenchglen and the Frenchglen Hotel.

NOTES

DAY NINE

FRENCHGLEN TO SILVER LAKE

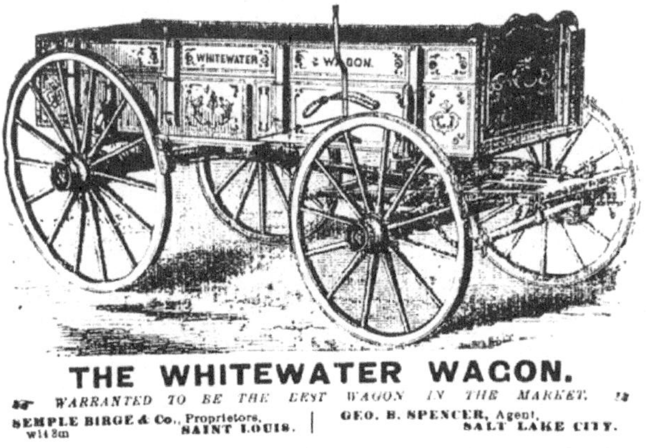

Day 9
Frenchglen to Silver Lake

Day 9 – Date: / /

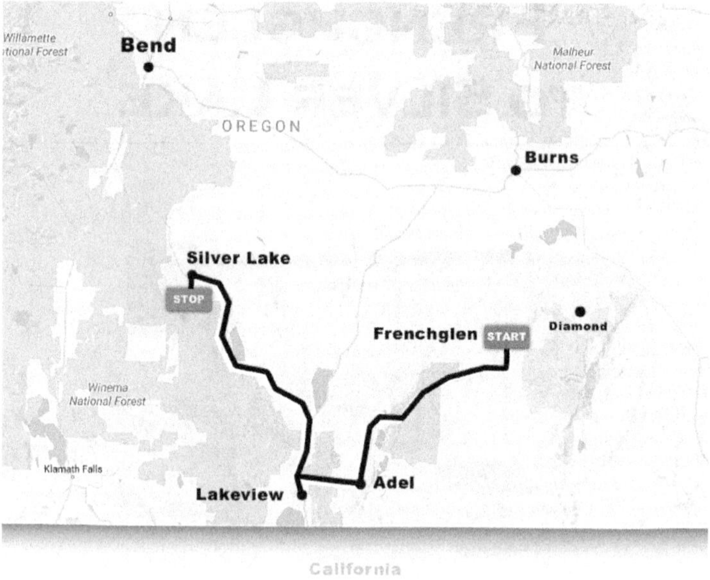

Summary: Where You're Going Today

- Frenchglen, OR
- Hart Mountain National Antelope Refuge
- Adel, OR
- Lakeview, OR
- Summer Lake State Wildlife Area
- Silver Lake, OR

Today's journey continues west through the open expanse of the Hart Mountain National Antelope Refuge to Adel, OR, where you'll have lunch at a restaurant you normally wouldn't stop at, but you'll be so glad you did. From here, you'll continue to the small town of Plush before reaching Lakeview and turning north on the Oregon Outback Scenic Byway toward Silver Lake.

Here, you'll enjoy a very memorable meal at the Cowboy Dinner Tree Restaurant before sleeping in your cabin under an abundance of stars.

Tonight's Lodging:

- Cowboy Dinner Tree Restaurant & Lodging
- Or 3 lodging options - See page 161

Today's Mileage: 224 Miles

Reservations Needed for This Segment:

- Cowboy Dinner Tree Restaurant & Lodging - You will be making reservations for 1 night of lodging. In addition, we highly recommend you make reservations for dinner. See page 158 for details - 541-576-2426

Before You Leave:

Fill your gas tank before leaving Frenchglen.

First Stop: Hart Mountain National Antelope Refuge

Leaving Frenchglen, you soon begin to traverse the large Hart Mountain National Antelope Refuge, and the odds of seeing a beautiful American Pronghorn Antelope greatly increase. Keep your eye out for herds or single Pronghorns, which can be anywhere, including lying on the road you're traveling. *Photo © Tom Koerner/USFWS*

Note: In addition to Pronghorn Antelope, Bighorn Sheep can be seen year-round. Because you are unlikely to see them with the naked eye, it is best to use binoculars. Search for them at the base of Hart Mountain, from the Refuge Headquarters or any other location along the road.

Driving Directions: From the Frenchglen Hotel - Drive south on Hwy 205 for 6.8 miles to Rock Creek Ln./Rd. Turn right here, at the sign that reads, *Hart Mt Refuge 37*, and drive west. Rock Creek Ln. continues for 22.5 miles, where it meets the eastern edge of the Hart Mountain National Antelope Refuge. At this point, while remaining the same road, it becomes Frenchglen Rd.

Note: The main road through the Hart Mountain National Antelope Refuge tends to remain open all year, but can be closed temporarily by extreme weather conditions in the winter. For questions regarding current road conditions, call the Refuge Headquarters at 541-947-2731.

Next Stop: Hart Mountain National Antelope Refuge Headquarters

As you make your way west along the main road through the refuge, you'll come upon the refuge headquarters, a small collection of stone buildings, which used to be a CCC camp in the 1930s. The main structure houses a small unmanned visitor center, which is open 24/7. Inside, you'll find a small room with displays, photos, and a handful of artifacts from the refuge, including skulls, bones, teeth and more. A restroom is also available here.

Hart Mountain National Refuge Headquarters
38782 Hart Mountain Road
Plush, OR 97637

Note: The headquarter's address shows it is located in Plush, OR, but it is actually 23.5 miles northeast of Plush.

Driving Directions: You will automatically arrive at the Hart Mountain National Antelope Refuge Headquarters while traveling on Frenchglen Road, 41 miles after leaving Hwy 205 and nearly 48 miles after leaving the Frenchglen Hotel. Note: Frenchglen Road becomes Hart Mountain Road immediately south of the Hart Mountain National Antelope Refuge Headquarters.

Next Stop: Petroglyph Lake Hike

Hike far into Oregon's past and discover a collection of ancient petroglyphs depicting many intriguing figures. This is an excellent opportunity to get an up close look at this ancient art form in its original context. However, please be sure to not touch or disturb the images.

Driving Directions: Proceed northwest on Hart Mountain Road from the headquarter offices for one mile. Here, you'll spot a small sign on the side of the road pointing toward Petroglyph Lake. Turn right onto this road, provided it is dry, and follow it for approximately 1.5 miles to a turnaround area. Note that the road is fine for passenger cars in the beginning, but becomes rougher near the turnaround. Park here and hike the obvious trail north for approximately 1/2 mile to a band of basalt cliffs on the west side of Petroglyph Lake. Follow well worn paths in the grass to the petroglyphs. Note: We followed paths to the south end of the cliffs, but did not find any petroglyphs until the next section of cliffs to the north.

Next Stop: Adel Store & Gas - Adel, Oregon

You can take a shortcut from Plush to Lakeview, but you won't want to, because that means you'll miss lunch at the Adel Store. Founded in 1896, this classic restaurant embodies the Oregon Outback and life in the southern edge of our state. Inside, you'll find an abundance of stuffed big game adorning the walls, saddles and branding irons hanging from the ceiling, and one of the best burgers you've had in a long time. In addition, they offer grilled sandwiches, pizza, tacos, ice cream and more.

Adel Store
18586 Twenty Mile Road
Hwy 140 E.
Adel, OR 97620
541-947-3851

Driving Directions: From the turnoff to Petroglyph Lake, continue west on Hart Mountain Road 22 miles to where it connects to Hogback Road, just north of the town of Plush, OR. Turn left/south onto Hogback Road and follow it through Plush. As you leave Plush, Hogback Road turns to head west for 0.3 miles before turning south. Follow Hogback Road south for 17.5 miles from this point until it comes to Hwy 140, directly across from the restaurant, gas station and Post Office that is Adel, OR.

Next Stop: Lakeview, Oregon

Located at an elevation of 4,798' on the edge of the southeast Oregon High Desert, Lakeview is the "Tallest Town in Oregon." You'll find many convenient services here, including a grocery store, cafes, restaurants, hardware stores, a hospital, a Les Schwab Tire Center, and Junipers Reservoir RV Resort. *Photo © Orygun*

Fill your gas tank before leaving Lakeview.

Driving Directions: From Adel, drive west on Hwy 140 for 28 miles to where it connects with Hwy 395 / The Oregon Outback Scenic Byway. Turn left/south and follow this 6 miles into Lakeview, OR.

Next Stop: Schminck Memorial Museum

Housed in a 1920s era bungalow, the Schminck Memorial Museum is home to over 5,000 pieces, including pioneer artifacts, quilts, native American items and more.

Schminck Memorial Museum
128 South E St.
Lakeview, OR 97630
541-947-3134

- Open February - November 10:00 a.m. - 4:00 p.m.
- Fee: $4.00 Donation

Driving Directions: As you drive south into Lakeview, look for S. 1st Street, (Not N. 1st Street) four blocks after passing Safeway. Turn left/east onto S. 1st Street and then turn right/south onto South E Street.

Next Stop: Lake County Museum

This small 1927 bungalow just down from the Schminck Memorial Museum showcases the history of Lake County. Inside, visitors will find historical cultural items, as well as genealogy research materials, including old photographs, papers, records, obituaries and marriage documents.

Lake County Museum
118 South E St.
Lakeview, OR, 97630
541-947-2220

- Open May 1 - October 31
- Thursdays - Saturday
- 12:00 p.m. - 4:00 p.m.

Directions: The museum is next door to the Schminck Museum.

Next Stop: Lake County Visitor Center

An excellent resource for information about Lake County. Stop in for maps, brochures, and advice on activities, restaurants, annual events and more.

Lake County Visitor Center
126 North E St.
Lakeview, OR
541-947-6040

- Open Thursday - Saturday, 12:00 p.m. - 4:00 p.m.

Driving Directions: Simply proceed north on North E Street to the Visitor Center.

Next Stop: MC Chuckwagon Western Heritage Exhibit

You've probably never been to a museum like this. Instead of entering the museum itself, guests walk around its exterior on a covered porch, moving from one large window to the next as they learn the story of the importance of the MC Chuckwagon, as well as the workings of the enormous MC Ranch, one of Oregon's largest cattle ranches at nearly one million acres.

MC Chuckwagon Western Heritage Exhibit
429 North F St.
Lakeview, OR 97630

- 541-947-2029 - Call for a personal tour.
- Open 24 Hours, 7 Days a Week - Free of charge

Driving Directions: Proceed north on F Street / Hwy 395 through the center of town. You'll find the MC Chuckwagon Western Heritage Exhibit one block north of Safeway, opposite the Les Schwab Tire Center.

Next Stop: Summer Lake Wildlife Area

Comprised of a large marsh within an 18,700 acre protected refuge, the Summer Lake Wildlife Area is one of the best places in Oregon to see large and impressive migrating flocks of geese, swans and ducks, (March - April) as well as countless waterbirds and songbirds. (April - May) Tour the Wildlife Area via an 8.3 mile tour route, which takes you to numerous stops and viewing areas throughout the Wildlife Area. *Photo © ODF&W*

- A Daily Parking Permit ($10) is required if you plan to park along the tour route, which is very likely.
- Parking permits may be purchased at the Summer Lake Wildlife Area Headquarters or Summer Lake Store.
- The 8.3 mile tour route may be accessed at the Summer Lake Wildlife Area Headquarters or Summer Lake Store/Thousand Springs Ln. opposite the store.
- Maps and a bird checklist are available at the headquarters location, but not the store.
- The tour route is closed in early October through late January.

Summer Lake Wildlife Area Headquarters
53447 Hwy 31
Summer Lake, OR 97640
541-943-3152

Summer Lake Store
37850 Hwy 31
Summer Lake, OR 97640
541-943-3164

(1.3 Miles north of the Summer Lake Wildlife Area Headquarters and The Summer Lake Lodge)

Driving Directions: From the MC Chuckwagon Western Heritage Exhibit in Lakeview, proceed north on the Oregon Outback Scenic Byway / Hwy 395 for 22.5 miles to the junction of Hwy 395 and Hwy 31. Proceed north onto Hwy 31 and follow this 50 miles to the Summer Lake Wildlife Area Headquarters on the right, opposite The Summer Lake Lodge.

Begin the 8.3 mile tour route at the Summer Lake Wildlife Area Headquarters or proceed 1.3 miles north to the Summer Lake Store and begin opposite the store, on Thousand Springs Ln.

TONIGHT'S LODGING - COWBOY DINNER TREE RESTAURANT & LODGING

It's old and rustic, very remote, hardly known...and always busy.

The last night of your road trip finishes at the Cowboy Dinner Tree Restaurant & Lodging. Welcoming families, friends and folks of all kinds, this Oregon High Desert Icon resides in a low slung shack of a building filled with artifacts from Oregon's cattle ranching history. For dinner, you can choose one of only two entrees...a *26 - 30 oz. Top Sirloin steak* or *one whole roasted chicken.* Yes, those numbers are correct! Oh, and a baked potato, freshly made rolls, a salad and soup. No splitting dinners! The good news is that you can take leftovers with you. Though remote, the restaurant is usually busy, so reservations are required.

Dinner:

- $45 per person - Ages 7-13 are $11 each - 6 and under are free - No splitting dinners.
- *No credit cards, no debit cards, no checks - CASH ONLY.*

Lodging:

Photo © Gary Muncy

The Oregon High Desert experience continues with your lodging, as four comfortable cabins offer clean rooms with full amenities for road trippers, cyclists, motorcyclists and even cowboys moving the herd up yonder. All you need are your personal items.

- Cabin occupancy varies from 2 to 7
- $100 - $150 per night for two
- $25 - $50 per extra person
- Pets are not allowed
- *NOTE: CASH ONLY*

Cowboy Dinner Tree Restaurant & Lodging
50962 E Bay Road
Silver Lake, OR 97638

www.CowboyDinnerTree.net

Dinner & Lodging Reservations: 541-576-2426

- Make your dinner reservations at least one month in advance during the spring, summer and fall months.
- The cabins are usually booked 3 to 6 months in advance, but last-minute openings do occur. It is best to call sooner, rather than later.

Restaurant Hours: Open year round - Hours vary by season

- June 1st - October 31st: 4:00 p.m. - 7:30 p.m. - Thursday, Friday, Saturday & Sunday
- Nov. 1st - May 31st: 4:00 p.m. - 7:30 p.m. - Friday, Saturday & Sunday
- *No credit cards, no debit cards, no checks - CASH ONLY.*

Photos © TripAdvisor

Driving Directions: The Cowboy Dinner Tree Restaurant & Lodging is 101 miles from Lakeview, OR.

From the Summer Lake State Wildlife Area Headquarters, proceed north and then northwest on the Oregon Outback Scenic Byway / Hwy 31 for 23 miles to E. Bay Road in Silver Lake, OR. (96 Miles from Lakeview) Turn left/south off of Hwy 31 onto E. Bay Road and follow this for 4.5 miles to the Cowboy Dinner Tree Restaurant & Lodging on your right.

BTW, we haven't eaten there for breakfast, but based on their menu...and their cinnamon rolls... the **Silver Lake Café & Bar** at 65320 Hwy 31 in Silver Lake looks like a nice place to start your day.

Lodging Options

Lodging options in this part of the state are a bit dispersed, so note their locations when making any reservations.

Lodging Option #1: Summer Lake Hot Springs

With a history reaching back to 1926, Summer Lake Hot Springs looks out over 145 acres and offers travelers six newly renovated cabins, as well as two newly built duplexes, all with queen beds, private baths, kitchenettes, heated floors, and a "TV-free environment." In addition, you'll find full RV hookups and tent camping sites. Note that the cabins and duplexes require a two night minimum. Post Covid-19, guests must provide their own bedding.

Summer Lake Hot Springs
41777 Highway 31
Paisley, OR 97636
541-943-3931

Driving Directions: Summer Lake Hot Springs is 51 miles northwest of Lakeview, OR. From the MC Chuckwagon Western Heritage Exhibit in Lakeview, proceed north on the Oregon Outback Scenic Byway / Hwy 395 for 22.5 miles to the junction of Hwy 395 and Hwy 31. Proceed north onto Hwy 31 and follow this 28 miles to Summer Lake Hot Springs.

Lodging Option #2: Hunter's Hot Springs Resort

Two miles north of Lakeview is Hunter's Hot Springs Resort. Located on the site of natural geothermal hot springs, the resort offers 20 rooms, free Wi-Fi and TVs, as well as small refrigerators and microwaves.

Hunter's Hot Springs Resort
18088 US-395
Lakeview, OR 97630
541-947-4242

Driving Directions: From the MC Chuckwagon Western Heritage Exhibit in Lakeview, proceed north on the Oregon Outback Scenic Byway / Hwy 395 for 1.9 miles to Hunter's Hot Springs Resort.

Lodging Option #3: The Lodge at Summer Lake

Located on Hwy 31, at the base of Winter Rim and opposite the Summer Lake State Wildlife Area, The Lodge at Summer Lake offers pet friendly lodge rooms, as well as newly built and fully equipped cabins overlooking its stocked three acre pond. In addition, the Flyaway Restaurant serves steaks, seafood, burgers with homemade buns, chicken plates, salads, desserts and more.

The Lodge at Summer Lake
53460 Highway 31
Summer Lake, OR 97640
541-943-3993

Driving Directions: From the MC Chuckwagon Western Heritage Exhibit in Lakeview, proceed north on the Oregon Outback Scenic Byway / Hwy 395 for 22.5 miles to the junction of Hwy 395 and Hwy 31. Proceed north onto Hwy 31 and follow this 50 miles to The Lodge at Summer Lake on the left.

Notes

DAY TEN

COWBOY DINNER TREE TO HOME

Day 10
Cowboy Dinner Tree to Home

Red-Tailed Hawk - Near Valley Falls, Oregon

Day 10 – Date: / /

Summary: Where You're Going Today

- Cowboy Dinner Tree Restaurant & Lodging
- Crack in the Ground
- Green Mountain Fire Lookout & Campground
- Fort Rock
- Fort Rock Homestead Village Museum
- Hole in the Ground
- Home

Today, your Southeast Oregon road trip comes to a close, but not without a day of discovering even more Oregon history and scenic wonders.

You'll begin by traveling to the small town of Christmas Valley, where the street names all have a holiday flair, before continuing north and then back west, where you'll immerse yourself in some unique and amazing Oregon geology.

Before You Leave:

Fill your gas tank in Silver Lake or Christmas Valley after leaving Cowboy Dinner Tree.

First Stop: Crack in the Ground

At over two miles in length and up to 70' deep, Crack in the Ground certainly lives up to its name. This unique geological wonder features towering basalt walls that at times are so close together you can reach out and touch each side at once.

Crack in the Ground consists of sections in which you "drop down" into the crack and hike a ways before popping out again at the other end, only to repeat the process with the next section. Along the rim of the crack is a trail, which runs its distance. Because some sections of the crack contain rock fall, which requires climbing, route-finding and back tracking, we recommend hiking the first segment, hiking the rim trail along the second and third segments, and then dropping back down and hiking the crack through the fourth segment. You can then either back track the way you came, or hike the entire rim trail back to the main trail to your car.

Note: Some areas of the Crack in the Ground are easily hiked, but others require a bit of courageous down climbing and are unsuitable for young children.

Driving Directions: From the town of Silver Lake, drive east on Hwy 31 for 3 miles to Arrow Gap Road. Turn left/north onto Arrow Gap Road and follow this for 7.6 miles to Christmas Valley - Wagontire Rd. Turn right/east here and follow this for 12 miles to the east end of Christmas Valley, where you'll see a sign that reads "Crack in the Ground 7.5 Miles". Turn left/north onto Crack in the Ground Road and follow this to an obvious parking lot, restroom and kiosk at the *7.0* mile mark. The wide trail for Crack in the Ground starts across from the parking lot, heading east. There is no fee to park here.

Next Stop: Green Mountain Fire Lookout & Campground

Following the same road you took for Crack in the Ground, but to the 12.6 mile mark, you'll find the Green Mountain Fire Lookout Tower and its corresponding campground. Open during the spring, summer and fall, the lookout tower will often welcome visitors up in the viewing area, where they'll get a stunning 360 degree view of the Christmas Valley and Fort Rock area from 5,190', which most Oregonians never see. If the tower is closed and you cannot access it, there is still a very impressive view available from its base.

Note: The campground here offers six of some of the most scenic campsites found in the state, but services are limited to picnic tables, fire grates and a vault toilet. Potable water is not available.

Fire Lookout Hours of Operation:

- 9:30 a.m. - 6:00 p.m. Memorial Day Weekend to Mid-September
- 8:00 a.m. - 4:00 p.m. Mid-September to October
- Closed in Winter

Driving Directions: Proceed 5.6 miles beyond the parking area for Crack in the Ground (12.6 Miles total from the highway) to the campground and fire lookout.

Next Stop: Fort Rock

A massive geological feature towering 200' over the high desert landscape, Fort Rock is an impressive testament to the geological history of Central Oregon. Hike the loop trail through its inner crater to get a sense of its 4,460' circumference, as well as an up close view of its volcanic tuff walls inhabited by Cliff Swallows, Prairie Falcons, Great Horned Owls, Barn Owls, Bald Eagles and more.

Stop at the interpretive board to get information on the 1.1 mile inner loop trail, which makes its way up into the crater. Note: This can be a hot hike in July and August.

Driving Directions: Return on Crack in the Ground Road to where it connects with Christmas Valley - Wagontire Rd. Turn right/west and follow this west for 12 miles. Then turn right and follow what is now Fort Rock Road as it executes a series of right and left hand turns before reaching Cabin Lake Road at 28 miles. Turn right/north onto Cabin Lake Road and proceed 1.5 miles to the obvious Fort Rock State Park.

Next Stop: Fort Rock Homestead Village Museum

What began with two buildings in 1988 is now an entire historical village made up of a church, school, offices, homes, a blacksmithing shop and a grocery store, all surrounded by vintage farm equipment and depicting the difficult lives of the early homesteaders and their quest to establish a home in the high desert.

The Reception Center offers interpretive displays, restrooms and a small gift shop.

Driving Directions: Return via Cabin Lake Road to Fort Rock Hwy / County Hwy 5-10, and proceed west 0.1 mile to the Fort Rock Homestead Village Museum on the left.

Next Stop: Home

With its capturing of the many different facets of Oregon's historical old west, the Fort Rock Homestead Village Museum makes an excellent point at which to end your Southeast Oregon road trip.

We hope you greatly enjoyed discovering and enjoying the amazing geological, historical, cultural and scenic wonders of our beautiful state, and that you had the opportunity to create many wonderful memories to tide you over until your next Oregon road trip!

Our Recommendations on How to Travel Home:

If you're heading home toward **Portland** and points north, we recommend you leave Fort Rock and drive northwest on the Oregon Outback Scenic Byway / Hwy 31 to where it connects with Highway 97, just south of La Pine. Then follow this north to where it joins Hwy 26 in Madras, OR and continue over Mt. Hood.

If you're heading toward **Central Oregon, Southern Oregon or the Willamette Valley**, then you'll want to continue northwest on the Oregon Scenic Byway / Hwy 31 to where it connects with Hwy 97, just south of La Pine, OR.

Bonus Stop: Hole in the Ground

If you're heading home and you want to make one more "bonus" stop that is conveniently located on your way, then we suggest Hole in the Ground. Another geologic wonder of this area and one most Oregonians have never seen, the interesting Hole in the Ground resembles an impact crater from a meteor, but it was actually forged from the earth by a massive volcanic explosion, which created a "hole" one mile wide and 490' deep. Drive to its western edge to get a good look at its size.

Driving Directions: As you travel northwest toward La Pine, OR on the Oregon Outback Scenic Byway / Hwy 31, turn right/north onto NF Rd. 3125, a gravel and dirt road across from Mile Post 22. *Reset your odometer here.* Stay to the right at the first "Y" at 0.1 mile, and then at 3.1 miles (not the turn at 3.0!) turn right onto NF Rd. 3130, which is unmarked. Continue for 1.2 miles to NF Rd. 200, and then turn left here and proceed 0.1 mile to the dirt parking area.

Phone Numbers - Oregon Road Trips - Southeast Edition

- Cowboy Dinner Tree Restaurant & Lodging: 541-576-2426
- Fields Station - Fields, OR: 541-495-2275
- Flat Iron Steak House & Inn - Jordan Valley: 541-586-2800
- Frenchglen Hotel: 541-493-2825
- Frenchglen Mercantile: 541-493-2564
- Hart Mountain Antelope Refuge - Road Info: 541-947-2731
- Historic Hotel Diamond: 541-493-1898
- Historic Hotel Prairie: 541-820-4800
- Hunter's Hot Springs: 541-947-4242
- Jordan Valley Gas Station: 541-586-2244 - Open 24 Hours
- Kam Wah Chung State Heritage Site: 541-575-2800
- Les Schwab Tire Center - Burns: 541-573-2015
- Les Schwab Tire Center - John Day: 541-575-1346
- Les Schwab Tire Center - Madras: 541-475-3834
- Les Schwab Tire Center - Nampa, Idaho: 208-467-2127
- Les Schwab Tire Center - Nampa, Idaho: 208-468-4121
- Les Schwab Tire Center - Prineville: 541-447-5686
- Leslie Gulch - BLM Office - Vale, OR: 541-473-3144
- Malheur National Wildlife Refuge: 541-493-2612
- Pine Shadows Getaway - Prairie City: 541-820-3736
- Service Creek Stage Stop: 541-468-3331
- Steens Mountain Tour Loop - Road Info: 541-573-4400
- Steens Mountain Wilderness Resort: 800-542-3765
- Summer Lake Hot Springs: 541-943-3931
- Summer Lake Store: 541-943-3164
- Summer Lake Wildlife Area: 541-943-3152
- The Lodge at Summer Lake: 541-943-3993

A Northeast Oregon Road Trip!

Oregon Road Trips - Northeast Edition

Now discover Northeast Oregon's scenic backroads and byways by day, *while staying in historic hotels by night!*

With our *Oregon Road Trips - Northeast Edition* guide, you'll explore the scenic beauty of Northeast Oregon while you ride aboard a historic steam train, wander Oregon ghost towns, ascend in a cable tram to over 8,000', stay at the 1907 Balch Hotel, board the Sumpter Valley Dredge, explore Cottonwood Canyon, ride the rails on a 2-seater, explore unique shops, eat at great restaurants, meet friendly people and so much more!

An adventurous Northeast Oregon road trip awaits, and it's already planned for you!

Available at Retailers Throughout Oregon, Discover-Oregon.com and Online

Now Enjoy An Oregon Coast Road Trip!

Oregon Road Trips - Oregon Coast Edition

Pack your bags, because you're about to explore the grandeur of Oregon's dramatic coastline during an adventurous 9-day road trip from Astoria south to Brookings. You'll journey along Oregon's beautiful Highway 101 as you discover countless scenic beaches, tour historic lighthouses, wander through quaint beach towns, watch whales spouting just off shore, ride in the cab of a 1925 steam locomotive, eat tasty Dungeness Crab fresh off the boat...or catch your own, stay in historic hotels, explore unique shops, meet friendly people and so much more!

Your perfect Oregon Coast road trip awaits!

Available at Retailers Throughout Oregon,
Discover-Oregon.com and Online

Discover the Columbia River Gorge!

Oregon Road Trips – Columbia River Gorge Edition

Journey along the Historic Columbia River Highway deep into the Columbia River Gorge, where you'll spend five days seeing the Gorge's majestic waterfalls, flying in a vintage 2-seater biplane, hiking through the historic Mosier Tunnels, stepping into the void on an exciting zip line tour, walking amidst the Gorge's beautiful spring wildflowers, finding your next book at Oregon's oldest bookstore, and even spotting Giraffes, Zebras, Camels, Ostriches and more!

Your Columbia River Gorge road trip awaits, and it's already planned for you!

Available Now at Retailers Throughout Oregon, Discover-Oregon.com and Online

ROAD TRIP OREGON'S MAJESTIC MT. HOOD!

Oregon Road Trips - Mt. Hood Edition
Via the Columbia River Gorge

An alpine Oregon Road Trip adventure is waiting for you!

Set out on an exciting Oregon road trip where every night ends at a charming historic hotel, finishing with majestic Timberline Lodge at 6,000' on the south slope of Mt. Hood! Explore the Historic Columbia River Highway, hike the unique Mosier Tunnels route, visit Oregon's oldest bookstore, walk among the Columbia River Gorge's colorful spring wildflowers, fly in a vintage 2-seater biplane, ride to over 7,000' on the Magic Mile Chairlift, discover the rustic and remote 1889 Cloud Cap Inn on Mt. Hood's eastern flank, and so much more.

Available at Retailers Throughout Oregon, Discover-Oregon.com and Online

Discover All Of Central Oregon

Central Oregon is a big place. To the west, high Cascade lakes and snowy peaks offer a world of alpine adventure, while to the east, the high desert beckons travelers to another world, one filled with thrilling experiences and geological wonders. In between is a land of scenic vistas, majestic waterfalls, amazing attractions, and countless outdoor and indoor adventures just waiting to be explored, and they're all here for you in the new *Central Oregon - An Explorer's Guide!* Use this guide to discover **more than 200** unique attractions, destinations, and experiences where you'll discover nine thundering waterfalls, set out on a moonlight kayaking adventure, walk among WWII era aircraft, hike through Oregon's high desert, ride a summer chairlift up Mt. Bachelor to enjoy some amazing alpine views, drive to the top of Paulina Peak, watch world-class rock climbing up close, paddleboard and kayak on the slow flowing Deschutes River, explore an ancient lava tube, and much more!

Available Now at Retailers Throughout Oregon, Discover-Oregon.com and Online

ROAD TRIP WASHINGTON'S OLYMPIC PENINSULA

Washington's Olympic Peninsula has always been somewhat of a mystery, but now it's an adventurous and perfectly planned 6-day road trip! Set out to discover this exciting world that varies from high alpine peaks and lofty hiking trails to long sandy beaches and captivating ocean vistas. Stay at and explore the busy Victorian seaport of Port Townsend, visit a historic lighthouse, tour a vintage airplane museum, kayak on the Strait of Juan de Fuca, see majestic orcas, humpbacks, and gray whales, sleep in your very own castle, stand in the quietest place in the United States, explore unique shops, eat at great restaurants, meet friendly people, and so much more!

Your perfect Northern Olympic Peninsula road trip awaits...and it's already planned for you!

Available Now at Retailers Throughout Washington and Online

EXPLORE WASHINGTON'S OLYMPIC PENINSULA

Now easily discover over 150 things to see, do and explore on Washington's Northern Olympic Peninsula!

The majestic northern Olympic Peninsula is filled with scenic vistas, beautiful beaches, graceful waterfalls, amazing attractions, and countless adventures, and they're all waiting for you in the *Northern Olympic Peninsula - An Explorer's Guide.* Tour a vintage aeroplane museum, visit historic lighthouses, learn how wooden kayaks are made, sleep in your very own castle, see Orcas, Gray Whales, and Humpbacks up close, discover the most beautiful waterfall on the Olympic Peninsula, explore historic Fort Worden, hike stunning Shi Shi and Rialto beaches, hike the captivating Hoh Rainforest, wander old town Port Townsend, and so much more!

Available Now at Retailers Throughout Washington and Online

ABOUT THE AUTHORS

Mike & Kristy Westby

Having been to all six "corners" of Oregon...North, South, East, West, Top and Bottom, (The top of Mt. Hood and the Oregon Coast) we decided it would be fun to take off on a series of multi-day road trips throughout the state. During our travels, we were surprised at the number of folks we met along the way who told us that they've always wanted to do the same thing, but they didn't know where to even begin planning such a trip. How do you find interesting places? What routes do you take? How do separate it all into even days, all while ending each day at a historic hotel? With that in mind, we decided to write our road trip guides so other like-minded souls can easily benefit from the knowledge we've gleaned over the years and set out on their own adventures.

We'd love to hear about the journeys you've taken with our different road trip guides, so feel free to drop us a note anytime or send us a photo, especially if you're on the road!

ContactUs@Discover-Oregon.com

OREGON & 1

Oregon, we want to start a grass roots movement.

Imagine if every business in Oregon, large or small, huge or tiny, promoted *at least* one other Oregon business...at no charge, which is completely unrelated to their business.

- A small café promotes a bookstore on its menu.
- A bookstore promotes a historical carousel with a placard by the cash register.
- A historical carousel promotes a tour provider with a small sign near the ticket counter.
- A tour provider promotes a tire store with a mention on its brochures.
- A tire store promotes a local hotel with a note on its invoices.
- A local hotel promotes a theater in the next town over with current showtimes listed at its check-in counter.
- A local theater promotes an auto repair shop with a small sign on its door.
- An auto repair shop promotes a small café with a menu placed in the waiting room.

Creative opportunities to promote Oregon businesses are endless. Better yet, each requires *very little effort or expense* and can start right now...at your business. How do you decide who to promote? Let your employees pick their favorites and rotate their choices on a regular basis.

With all of us extending a hand to our fellow Oregonians

beginning today, we can build a powerful interconnected web that reaches all across the state and cross-promotes thousands and thousands of Oregon businesses every day, thus lifting our state's economy, adding to your neighbor's paycheck, and bringing more business to your business.

Oregon and 1!

We Recommend...

Restore Oregon

As you journeyed through Southeast Oregon, you no doubt noticed the old structures which capture the history and culture of our state. Many, however, are in urgent need of protection and preservation. Restore Oregon is dedicated to "taking care of the places that make Oregon, OREGON" and preserving them for future generations. Learn more at RestoreOregon.org

Arrowhead Chocolates

Located in Joseph, Oregon, at the base of the lofty Wallowa Mountains, Arrowhead Chocolates offers some of the finest hand-crafted chocolates you'll find in Oregon, or the world for that matter. Step through the door into their shop and you'll find a wide selection of award-winning truffles, caramels, toffees, barks and more, all made in small batches, with each piece tasting better than the last. The good news is you can have them shipped directly to you! Order yours at www.ArrowheadChocolates.com - 541-432-2871

Les Schwab Tire Centers

If you're on the road and have a flat tire, brake issues or a similar problem, we highly recommend the very helpful folks at your nearby Les Schwab Tire Center. Located throughout Oregon. You'll find phone numbers for a number of locations on page 172.

75 Classic Rides: Oregon

From an after-work ride through Portland's neighborhood streets or a family cycle along the flat Willamette Valley Scenic Bikeway, to a multi-day tour in the salty breezes of the Oregon coast—if you're seeking the best bike routes in Oregon, you'll find plenty to ride in Jim Moore's *75 Classic Rides: Oregon.*

The Nature of Bend

Written by Bend's own LeeAnn Kriegh, *The Nature of Bend* is a nature guide like no other. Funny, informative, and filled with local flavor, it's the one book you need to identify, learn about, and locate more than 350 plants and animals found across Central Oregon. Available at bookstores, coffee shops, grocery stores and other retailers. Also look for *The Nature of Portland.* Learn more at NatureofBend.com

Smith Rock Nut Roasters

Central Oregon's own Smith Rock Nut Roasters offers a mouth-watering collection of roasted nut treats, including roasted candied almonds, hazelnuts, and cashews, as well as salted toffee almonds, vanilla cardamom almonds, salted toffee cashews, and much more. Look for them at local retailers throughout Central Oregon.

Are You a Disneyland Fan?

Enjoy a fascinating and entertaining book which reveals **over 250** of the hidden secrets and story elements that the Disney Imagineers have purposely hidden for Disneyland guests to find and enjoy, complete with 225 photos!

Available online, as well as at the prestigious Walt Disney Family Museum, the Walt Disney Boyhood Home, and the Walt Disney Hometown Museum.

Want Even More Disneyland Secrets?

Discover the in-depth stories behind more than 50 magical story elements of Disneyland, *many of which are published here for the very first time.* Compiled from extensive research and lengthy interviews with Disney Legends, Imagineers, and other Disney notables.

Available online, as well as at the prestigious Walt Disney Family Museum, the Walt Disney Boyhood Home, and the Walt Disney Hometown Museum.

Are You a Walt Disney World Fan?

See and experience Walt Disney World in an entirely new way! Written by Oregon author Mike Fox, *The Hidden Secrets & Stories of Walt Disney World* reveals **over 500** of the fun and oftentimes whimsical secret story elements that the Disney Imagineers have hidden throughout all four parks. Complete with 400+ photos.

Available online, as well as at the Walt Disney Hometown Museum and the Walt Disney Boyhood Home.

Camp Attitude

"Changing lives one camper at a time!"

Camp Attitude provides a welcoming camp experience for disabled youth and their families. Here, children with special needs can participate in all of the fun, games, excitement and interaction of a thrilling week-long "summer camp" experience, all for a nominal fee, thanks to donations from contributors who enjoy seeing a smile on a child's face...and a squirt gun in their hand!

Camp Attitude is a faith-based non-profit organization, and donations may be made by visiting their web site at www.CampAttitude.org

Camp Attitude
PO Box 2017
45829 S Santiam Hwy
Foster, OR 97345
541-401-1052

www.DeschutesRiverPress.com

Made in the USA
Middletown, DE
27 June 2023

33820403R00106